BILL GOSSE

SCORE

Guide to Supporting and Instilling Exceptional Sportsmanship

TITLETOWN
PUBLISHING

SCORE

TitleTown Publishing, LLC
P.O. Box 12093 Green Bay, WI 54307-12093
920.737.8051 | titletownpublishing.com

Cover Designer: Erika L. Block
Developmental Editor: Erin Walton
Copy Editor: Cassidy Schwimmer

PUBLISHER'S CATALOGING-IN-PUBLICATION DATA:

Names: Gosse, Bill, author.
Title: Score : guide to supporting and instilling exceptional sportsmanship / Bill Gosse. Other titles: Sports Creates Opportunities to Respect and Encourage

Description: Green Bay, Wisconsin : TitleTown Publishing, [2022] | Series: SCORE ; book 1. | Audience: Parents and adults involved with youth athletes.

Identifiers: ISBN: 978-1-955047-10-4 (paperback) 978-1-955047-11-1 (eBook)

Subjects: LCSH: Sportsmanship--Study and teaching. | Sports for children--Moral and ethical aspects. | Sports for children--Social aspects. | Sports--Moral and ethical aspects. | Coaching (Athletics)--Moral and ethical aspects. | Athletes--Conduct of life. | Leadership.

Classification: LCC: GV706.3 .G67 2022 | DDC: 796.01--dc23

Vision – To develop a spirit in sport where victory is not measured so much on the scoreboard, as it is in the stands and on the benches; where children, teens and adults can celebrate victory or defeat with style, grace, and sportsmanship; developing character for success in life.

WHEN SPORTSMANSHIP PREVAILS, WE ALL SCORE!

TeamScore Inc is a non-profit organization on a mission to promote good sportsmanship in youth athletics.

President and Co-Founder Bill Gosse brings a unique perspective to the subject of sportsmanship: Currently the Executive Director at St. Vincent de Paul Green Bay; NCAA D1 walk-on in basketball; father of five grown boys; coach for several youth teams; WIAA official, and Weekly sportsmanship columnist. He has seen *all* sides of sports, and still appreciates the great things it offers. He is passionate about improving the fan – and participant – environment in sports today.

bgosse23@gmail.com | (920) 562-2949

Table of Contents

Dedication

To my late father Edgar Gosse, who was always there for me growing up, setting a wonderful example. Thanks Dad. I love you.

Acknowledgements

Whether it was through school or church events, athletic contests, piano or trumpet lessons, or the memorable family day trips, I don't know if Dad could have set a better example for me. The countless hours of 500 he used to play with us, and the amount of time he spent playing catch and pitching with me, left such an impression. As an only child and the product of a humble, rural beginning, his selfless example and lifelong mission to provide his family with something better than he had growing up, was truly a gift from God, and amazes me to this day. He helped me dream big, which included attending Marquette University, trying out for the Warriors basketball team, raising a large family, writing a newspaper column, and thinking about writing a book, to name a few.

For some time, a book was in my thought process, but I wasn't sure how to go about it, and it almost got lost in the proverbial closet. Thanks to encouragement from Dad, my wife Debbie, and our five boys, the dream of writing a book stayed alive, and has come true. In fact, having five boys who are twelve years apart from youngest to oldest, and with varying degrees of interest in sports, helped position me to even be in a situation to write a book.

Certainly, Dad and Mom helped me out as an athlete, and were great sounding boards as that part of life was navigated. To be a parent is a special honor, and to be a parent of sports kids is not something to be taken for granted. Not all kids are interested, or as interested, in sports as others might be, and it takes time and effort to plug into what they may want to derive from sports. A great deal was learned from coaching them and also trying to be their father at the same time, which can be difficult. As with any experience, the results would be better if a second opportunity was granted.

As a longtime high school football official, who also dabbled in basketball and baseball officiating, I gained an appreciation and awareness for what officials have to tolerate, and the understanding exists why there is such a shortage of reliable and qualified officials. While working with all kinds of officials, it was easy to conclude some did it just for the money, but the pleasure of working with officials who strove for excellence was a wonderful experience. As you may imagine, it's a special feeling and accomplishment to be awarded the opportunity to officiate a state football final – 3 times. The realization also came to pass, that the more we prepare as officials, the better we are at handling all aspects of that responsibility.

As our last son's time in youth sports nears the end, our tie to youth sports shifts again to hopefully becoming a true fan and enjoy sports for what they were always intended to be, and that's plain, old-fashioned fun. Of course, as grandparenting eventually becomes part of our lives, that investment of emotion could take place again. Prayerfully, the club environment doesn't completely take that special feeling of fun away from sports fans.

Certainly, completing a book doesn't go directly from dream to reality, but it takes many different experiences, encounters, and episodes to get there. Honestly, the first seeds of writing a book were probably planted when the privilege of writing a regular sportsmanship column for the Green Bay Press-Gazette was granted to me, because my fondest memories of school truly don't include enjoying any school-related writing assignments. With that being said, excerpts or portions of my previously published columns have been reprinted in this book with permission from the Green Bay Press-Gazette, and I've been informed many of my past columns remain available for purchase through the greenbaypressgazette. com archives. Not being a trained writer, to even think of writing a column, came forth with thanks to an edition of The Sheboygan Press, which was brought to my attention by my in-laws.

In that particular sports section, there were three separate articles involving sportsmanship. They weren't regular columns, but feature stories, covering different aspects of poor sportsmanship.

I thought they were great, but felt these "one-shot deals" weren't going to do a whole lot of good, because their sound message would wear off quickly. That day, a commitment was proclaimed to my family that the Green Bay Press-Gazette needed a regular sportsmanship column, and my journey began to seek out their high school beat writer and author of one of the three articles in that sports section, Scott Venci, to see if his employer would be willing to take on such a proposition.

Already trying to establish a sportsmanship initiative, being able to write a regular column would be a great addition to the program and getting to know Scott through officiating high school football, my quest towards becoming a columnist continued. Without remembering how long it took, and how many counteroffers were involved, but basically, by offering my services for free, and agreeing to provide a column without even having to provide a sample, my journey into about 250,000 northeast Wisconsin homes, and many more across the internet began. However, out of a long-established desire for excellence, there was no way my initial efforts were going to be simply submitted without having an expert first review my creations.

That's where Lois Maurer, who was a producer for Milwaukee Public Television at the time, was contacted. I got to know Lois by way of her reaching out to me and offering a helping hand, after seeing me a year earlier on a Milwaukee morning talk show. On that program, my efforts to improve the sportsmanship environment surrounding youth sports were featured. Thank you to Lois for providing great guidance during the early days of my column-writing. Your help provided great training wheels.

Obviously, the Green Bay Press-Gazette staff deserves tremendous gratitude for bearing with a novice writer, who simply wanted the opportunity to speak from the heart and be able to plant seeds of good sportsmanship. Thanks are extended to Scott Venci, who advocated for me, and Editor Mike Vandermause, who took a chance on a genuine rookie. Nonetheless, 493 columns, and almost ten years later, my column-writing journey was complete, which wasn't possible without the wonderfully loyal readers who reached out to the Green Bay Press-Gazette and to me, offering ideas, encouragement, and constructive criticism. It was an experience that will be cherished forever. That experience, and my speaking engagements across the country, paved the way for this book. However, who would be my publisher?

My employment as Executive Director for The Society of St. Vincent de Paul Green Bay, provides exposure to The Business News, a publication for Northeast Wisconsin. On several occasions, there were articles about publishing companies, but none of them truly caught my attention, until one day there was an article about Titletown Publishing. The owner of this organization was also fully immersed as the manager of the local 9-1-1 office, and had quite a story. Without completely reading the article, and in an effort to meet the owner of Titletown Publishing, attempts were made to reach out to The Business News by sending an email to the writer of the Titletown Publishing article. Upon receiving no response, a follow-up was delivered to the editor of The Business News, which returned an assurance that someone would contact me. When that didn't happen either, the decision was made to read the whole article, which led to the discovery in the remainder of the article that an editor with Titletown Publishing had worked with me at a prior employer. *I'll just call her!* This phone call led to a meeting that would change everything. Thank you Tracy Ertl and Erin Walton for your help, encouragement, and all-around mentorship. This project has been more enjoyable than imagined, and anticipation awaits for what the Lord has next for all of us.

Lastly, recognition is warranted for the individuals who were willing to be interviewed for this book. These people offered valuable content to support my thoughts, and the experience of interviewing them was indeed a pleasure. Therefore, a special thank you goes out to Tim Bannon, Scott Venci, Ryan Borowicz, Paul Ihlenfeldt, Ron Meikle, Robert Brooks, and Dennis Freels. Best wishes and continued success to all of you, in and outside of sports.

Foreword

The world of sports has long been a staple in communities no matter where you live. In fact, it speaks a universal language that we all can understand on some level no matter where we're from.

In his book, Bill Gosse focuses on character disciplines such as control, respect, humility, and patience in the arena of sports that will always withstand the test of time. Those who demonstrate these will prove to be victorious on and off the field.

This resource will create conversations as well as provide insight for both the participant and the fans. It is a guide to embrace applicable good sportsmanship truths, creating an atmosphere where we all can enjoy the experience to the utmost.

In this first book of the series, Bill has created solid reading that should be incorporated in sports organizations, formal and informal. I'm excited to watch the trajectory of his ground-breaking work and the impact of his entire future series!

– Robert Brooks, Athletes in Action Pro Ministry, NFL Chaplain

Introduction

Teddy Roosevelt was often quoted as saying, "Some are born great, some achieve greatness, and some have greatness thrust upon them." Roosevelt isn't credited as being the author of that quote – William Shakespeare is – but Teddy was smart enough to surround himself with those who were high achievers when deciding how to live his own life that led to becoming the 26th President of the United States of America.

As a young boy, it's easy to remember the time when my father introduced me to sports. However, being probably all of eight or nine years of age at the time, just having fun was all that mattered to me. Looking to achieve greatness in sports wasn't in my thought process, because what did that mean? Dad took an old five-gallon can and cut out the bottom, nailed it high above in our garage to an old piece of tackboard, and our first backboard and hoop had been created. Then, Mom and Dad bought a simple, multi-colored bouncing ball from a local department store, and our first "basketball" had arrived.

Was I born a great athlete? Would I achieve greatness? Would greatness be thrust upon me? At that young of an age, that wasn't understood, nor was it something my parents were worried about.

They weren't trying to groom the next Lew Alcindor or Jerry West. They were simply trying to provide me with a fun activity to experience. It would be discovered later that my father's mission was always to try and provide his children with more than what he had as a child. You're probably thinking an old can, tackboard, and a bouncy ball isn't a whole lot, and you're right. However, with that humble beginning, he was already providing more than what he had as an only child raised during the Great Depression on a small farm in the early twentieth century in rural Wisconsin. He lived a life of hard work, during a time when graduation from high school, let alone college, was a luxury, not an expectation. To be clear, the gift wasn't in the humble basketball "equipment" he provided, it was in the opportunity to spend time with my father – something my grandfather rarely did with my dad. This quality time evolved into a love for the purity of sports, as I was taught sportsmanship and fair play, qualities that aren't always present in today's me-first world of tremendous salaries and intense competition.

For parents of young athletes, there are some easy tips to remember, which will help smooth out the sports parent journey.

If we adjust our expectations to focus on how beneficial it is for our children to simply be participating, instead of on wins and losses, it will be a whole lot less stressful. Especially at a younger age, our goal should be for the kids to have enough fun to want to come back the next year. Kids will develop confidence through wins and will be challenged through losses – *if* they're having fun. As it turns out, both situations are great for kids to experience, and we, as parents, need to understand that fact.

Another great thing to know is that only a small minority of all athletes actually receive college scholarships when they get older. According to Jack Renkens, Founder and President of Recruiting Realities, less than one percent of high school student-athletes receive a fully funded Division I scholarship. Therefore, we need to stop pressuring our kids to excel to be recognized. Again, let them participate in a way so that they want to play again in the future because they had self-satisfaction and fun.

The greatest thing we can do to support our children athletes is to encourage them and their teammates. Studies vary on this ratio, but a typical standard between praise and criticism should be at least 5 to 1. If we're not able to meet at least that expectation, we'll be causing our kids undue stress.

Former Baltimore Orioles baseball player and Hall of Famer Cal Ripken, Jr. says we should return the games to the kids, allowing them to have fun on their terms. We should let them develop, let them learn, let them fail, and support them in a way that is calming. This allows for a positive environment for the kids to learn the game and grow.

One of the best ways to support our kids without getting all worked up, is to volunteer our time to their coaches or the program in which they play. They may not currently need a coach, but helping transport kids to games, bringing nutritious snacks, or helping take care of the officials at the games is a great way to get involved without trying to be a coach in the stands. It also helps us get to know the people involved with our kids and we'll realize the majority of coaches and officials are well-intentioned people looking to have fun, too. We'll also realize they are people deserving respect, just like us.

Lastly, we always need to display good sportsmanship. As we've seen, especially at the younger age levels, the games are supposed to be more about fun than competition. Sportsmanship of fans should never be in question, because it should all be about encouraging our kids, remember? Nonetheless, it only takes one emotional outburst to give yourself, your team, your community, and most importantly your child, a black eye of embarrassment, and it takes longer than you'd like for that black eye to go away.

Your example will be contagious, so make it a good one.

Chapter 1

Getting Started

When I decided I wanted to do something to help kids in youth sports, it was because I had a burn to stop the nonsense I had been witnessing. Our oldest three boys were young enough to be right in the middle of some of the chaos, and it seemed like it was getting worse instead of better. What I was seeing made me uncomfortable and I wanted to make a positive difference.

I was motivated to do something to help the kids, but then I got some of the same feelings others might get when they want to *take on the world,* as doubts emerged.

Self-talk questions ran through my head: *Was what I was witnessing really that bad? Was the unsportsmanlike behavior only in our little corner of the world? Who was I to speak out about the behavior of parents at a basketball game? What gave me the right to be able to demand fans to stop yelling at officials? I didn't have a doctorate in psychology, so what gave me the right to think I knew something better than others? What would draw people to stop and listen to what I had to say anyway?*

I was getting tugged in two directions, but the stronger pull was coming from the end of wanting to do something positive – anything, but *would I be doing the right thing? How would I know if I was making a difference? Who was I really trying to help? Who in youth sports needed to clean up their act the most? Why did I have this knot in my stomach?*

Those questions and emotions flooded over me, just like they would in some shape or form for anyone wanting to step out and make a positive effect on society. When anyone wants to accuse people of improper behavior and try to foster change, they're probably going to feel *something.* I sure did.

Obviously, I got past the doubts, but how? Action. It's as simple as that. Put together a plan on how you want to make a difference, and then put it into action. That cured me as long as I kept working at it. When lulls in my opportunities to keep going presented themselves, invariably I'd have self-doubt creep in again. How bad did I want to make a difference? That's what I had to keep asking myself.

While creating my plan, I felt I needed to make a solid first step, something that would support my feelings. I decided I'd proceed with a basic survey and collect information that would either support what my gut was telling me needed to be done, or it would make it very clear to me I was chasing something that didn't exist. I wanted to be sure. Therefore, with the help of a former work colleague who had access to another gentleman in the statistical collection arena, we designed a survey for athletic directors. Wisconsin high school athletic directors would know who's to blame at sporting events, right? (Like I didn't already know.) Obviously, they're on the front lines each and every day, and they should be able to speak right out and point the finger at the culprit(s), so we could fix the craziness we read and see too often. I wanted the survey to be unbiased and professionally done, so the results would be clear and obvious, making it painfully clear what I felt I already knew.

After conducting the first survey, I enjoyed poring over the data. However, having some statistical background, I knew one set of data wouldn't be credible. Therefore, if one survey was good, two of them surely had to lead to the conclusive answer. Was it obvious I was stalling?

These studies were designed to determine the quality of sportsmanship at school sporting events and the prevalence of incidents of poor sportsmanship. The goal was to pinpoint problem areas, so that specific poor sportsmanship behaviors could be addressed and improved.

I didn't want to venture out on something that was a knee-jerk reaction, and what better way to justify a hunch than with statistical proof.

One question asked the respondents to identify three primary reasons for poor sportsmanship at school sporting events. The most frequent answer? Parents. *Tada!* Honestly, it wasn't a surprise to me parents were the main thorn in school leaders' sides, as well as the kids', and the officials'.

The surveys got me on my way, but I'd like to describe the experiences that put me over the edge to want to do something from the very beginning.

I have to admit, I'm as competitive as they come, and my own sportsmanship needs to be reeled in from time to time. In fact, I received a technical foul as a middle school basketball coach for yelling, "Holy moly!" at the officials. I didn't believe that I had actually cursed at the officials, but I disrespectfully raised my voice and didn't set a very good example for the kids I was trying to teach. I deserved the punishment because I had crossed the emotional line that so many people fail to recognize.

Dennis Freels of Keller, Texas, owner of GTTS LLC, an organizer of youth sports tournaments, uniform manufacturer, husband, and father, obviously has had experience working with other parents of children in sports. In fact, after dealing with parents quite a bit, he's formed some opinions, and laid them out when he told me, "I know it's a little embarrassing, but I've spent a lot of my time talking my son out of playing any sport, because I want him to understand it's (playing sports) not something you have to do in order to be successful. It's not something that life is all about. I was just so down on sports, because of the time I spent running youth tournaments, and the beating I took from some of the parents. They just turned me off so bad, I didn't want to have anything to do with youth sports. There are parents who can play so dirty, as they'll cause you grief, then they'll spin it, and then take it public. Even though I ran tournaments thirty-five weekends out of the year, I didn't want my family to participate in the very activity I worked. It's weird, but as a child, I felt I had to be in every sport. In fact, I had to have some event or competition coming up, just to get me through the week, or I felt inadequate."

In my own experiences as a sports parent leading up to launching my sportsmanship initiative, I observed what I viewed as bizarre behavior at sporting events. Because I strongly felt youth sports was (and still is) a great tool for teaching kids how to have fun, as well as other life lessons, the following events played a big role in steering me in the direction of trying to make a positive difference.

Three particular cases stick out in my head:

I witnessed one parent berating two basketball officials so extensively during an off-season tournament game, that the more-experienced official decided to take the initiative to stop the game and respectively go over to the stands and insist the father start acting as an adult, or he would be asked to leave. I also saw a mother choking her son at a youth wrestling tournament so he wouldn't cry because he lost his match. Include that with witnessing another father micromanaging his son's Gus Macker 3-on-3 Tournament team to the point where he stood with his toes right up to the out-of-bounds line as if those boys wouldn't be able to do anything without him dictating each and every move.

Sports aren't nearly as fun for kids when they must deal with parents like the ones I witnessed. These parents motivated me to try to make a difference through school and public presentations, television and radio appearances, magazine articles, newspaper columns, and now through this book.

As I recall the three aforementioned motivational scenarios, the situation where the veteran official confronted the loudmouth father excites me the most. Why? Because he followed through and made a positive difference not only in that man's life, but also in all the kids and people around that man who were adversely affected by his unacceptable behavior.

On that particular day, my family was visiting the tournament to watch our niece play. To get to the location where her game was being played, we had to pass through the gym where this incident took place. I remember pausing, watching, and being drawn into the whole situation as it unfolded with the official and the father. As a longtime high school football official, I could relate to this referee, and I could feel myself getting upset by the loudmouth parent. To this day, I know the official did the right thing, and I was fired up by his courage. I also realized why I didn't pursue basketball officiating further – the fans were too close.

In the episode at the youth wrestling tournament, I couldn't say anything to the mother choking her son, because I was so taken aback by her actions it caused me to freeze in my tracks. I had never seen anything like that before. Was there anything I could have done? Certainly. Looking back, I wish I asked her the simple question, "Is everything all right, ma'am?" Reaching out with that simple question may have helped her realize others were noticing that what she was doing was inappropriate, even though she was afraid her son would embarrass her because he lost a simple wrestling match at a youth tournament. She was hurting him, and I was selfishly worried about how she would respond to me, instead of stepping forward and doing the right thing. If I had asked her that question, I believe I would have been putting myself in a position of caring for that family – of simply trying to help, which is exactly what that boy and mother needed at that moment. Similar to the case of the basketball official, this moment of seed planting required an act of courage, which I wasn't able to muster at the time.

Regarding the other father, this was a time in those boys' lives where weekend 3-on-3 hoops tournaments should be more about having fun than being micromanaged by someone trying to resurrect his own playing days as he attempted to live through his child and a few friends. He managed those boys so extensively, my only remaining question was whether he followed them into the bathroom and dictated their every move in there, too. Again, I didn't say anything in that situation, and now that young son must be in his early twenties. I missed my opportunity at the time it was taking place, probably thinking more of how the father would react, instead of focusing on trying to help.

I understand we won't be able to change everyone, but we need to keep planting positive seeds. If enough people call out these unacceptable behaviors in a caring way and plant positive seeds of how sportsmanship should be conducted, our world will be a better place.

Sometimes no results will come, because the people might not understand what's being taught. For some, the positive effect might be followed with temporary excitement and then wither away. Others might hear what is said, but will worry about what others think, instead of making the necessary adjustments.

As seed planters, the results typically will never be known, and it shouldn't be our concern to know what will happen next. Sometimes the outcome might come full circle a year later, but most of the time the results of our positively planted seeds will be beneficial for someone else to enjoy. Let's be honest, not all of our seed-planting will be received positively. Nonetheless, if we want to make a positive difference, we must continue onward with examples reflective of our intent. Obviously, it will be a huge encouragement when we know some positive seeds take root and help others find their way. You can do the same thing. It just takes loving, caring action.

Chapter 2

Control

COVID-19 has had a great effect on our world. It's been a scary time for many people because they feel control has been lost to an invisible virus. When you study history, pandemics are viewed as a once-in-a-lifetime experience, and COVID-19 is being viewed as a pandemic, because of the number of lives lost worldwide. Growing up, many of us were taught to control what you can, and let someone else worry about what's out of our control. However, when something like this hits, and loved ones die, or become deathly sick, people become emotionally involved. When it hits close to home, the tragedy really starts to matter. When it appears we can't control the situation ourselves, chosen methods of resolve can be questionable or suspect, and people get nervous. When people become too emotionally involved, they cross the imaginary line of control and do things they might regret later.

When the spread of COVID-19 started in China, then began to sweep through foreign countries, we in America were able to watch it from afar. As it continued to advance throughout Europe, it still wasn't a serious issue until it began to invade our country. As the number of cases multiplied, people became more emotionally involved, but not everyone was convinced of the right way to "fix" the situation presented by the virus. We've had viruses come before, so why was this one different? Even within the medical community, consistent responses were not being passed along.

How was this any different than other situations we experience on a daily basis? For instance, according to the National Safety Council, almost 400,000 injuries occur each year from accidents caused by texting while driving, as drivers are looking down to see what someone is trying to tell them. Texting while driving is six times more likely to cause an accident than driving drunk.[1]

As a society, we frown heavily on drunk driving, and have been cracking down on offenders for as long as innocent people have been killed by drunk drivers. People got emotionally involved and used that emotion to change laws – to drive a more positive outcome.

According to the CDC (Center for Disease Control)[2], over 600,000 deaths related to abortion occurred in 2016 alone. The emotional investment in ending abortion isn't nearly the same as it has been to end drunk driving, texting while driving, or the coronavirus. It goes to show, changes can be made – good or bad – if we want them bad enough.

As our society gets better at adjusting, lives and businesses are surviving. It is true, many other businesses have closed forever, and countless people lost their jobs. Nonetheless, people are instructed to control what we can.

In our country, this situation became reality, especially for sports fans, when the 2020 NCAA Men's Basketball Tournament was not held for the first time since World War II. March Madness is a staple springtime event for basketball fans, if not sports fans in general, to not only watch, but participate in traditionally through taking off work for the first two days of jam-packed games on television. Depending on regional locations, others might be able to attend some of the games, but most participate by way of printing off a copy of and completing the overall tournament bracket, so we can enter our family and/or office pool to see if we can guess who the eventual national champion will be.

Doing without March Madness was just one of the many things we've had to do without as we've weathered the effects of COVID-19. Conducting sports with no fans in the stands was an incredible thing to even have to consider. However, that's how seriously we've viewed this virus and it's caused us to step back and reevaluate things.

When we are forced to adjust to what could be a "new normal," we must look in the mirror, knowing things may never be the same. That can hurt.

Nonetheless, having things taken away from us has offered opportunities we may not have even thought of if COVID-19 hadn't come around. Winston Churchill was quoted as saying, "Never waste a good crisis."

With that in mind, I had never heard of conducting a Zoom meeting. Conference rooms had to be booked in advance to reserve a physical space to hash out what we felt couldn't be done unless we were sitting across the table from each other. Meetings could go on-and-on, and sometimes it seemed we'd schedule meetings just for the sake of meeting. I still think face-to-face meetings are best, but nowadays, it's become quite commonplace for numerous people to "gather" in a virtual setting, and accomplish as much, or more, with as many people, or more, than we could have the traditional meeting way – *and* in less time! If this is truly the case, we've become more efficient.

Virtually presenting a new program to one hundred people from around the region was something I never could have imagined within a conference room, but now the 4-minute mile has been broken again, so to speak. In other words, we've shown ourselves we can adapt to new ways, and that gives me hope for when live sports begin flowing again.

In fact, in an interview with Tim Bannon, former veteran journalist of the Chicago Tribune, Bannon told me how he was amazed by the fact that despite professional sports largely being shut down during the summer of 2020, youth sports tournaments generally continued despite the effects of COVID-19. Bannon, a 2020-2021 Fellow with the O'Brien Fellowship in Public Service Journalism at Marquette University, wrote an article special to the Milwaukee Journal Sentinel in September of 2020 stating how the youth sports industry in America has grown to be a $19 billion industry.[3] No wonder sports academies, travel teams, and existing sports tournament businesses tried to keep going, and new sports-focused schools continue to dot the landscape.

In the interview, Bannon stated how tournament organizers felt the need to continue their businesses during the pandemic, like any other business owner had to decide, but made some adjustments, like moving tournaments to states where activities were still permitted. Bannon continued by stating how the second reason club tournaments kept going was because the desire to play was strong, and parents drove the market. In other words, parents are willing to adjust and take risks, so their children can keep playing.

Like adjustments made during COVID-19, we can control ourselves at sporting events if we really want to, and if we're taught, or maybe even required to, we can properly behave in order to stay in attendance, or even attend in the first place. It comes down to how bad we want the poor sportsmanship to go away.

How bad do we want the parental pressure of student athletes to take a back seat to respect and encouragement? How bad do we want to reduce the number of kids that give up sports altogether, because they've had it rammed down their throats by parents trying to live vicariously through their children?

Obviously, sports are a great way to blow off steam after a hard day. However, blowing off steam in positive support for our kids, grandkids, or just the home team, is one thing and more beneficial than blasting officials, criticizing coaches, or being jealous of others' success. Why? It's invigorating instead of stress-filled, and it helps us stay behind the line of emotion.

We all know people who get emotionally involved watching sports. Uniting in positive cheers for our favorite team is fun and enjoyable. It's unfortunate, but at times, too much negative yelling takes place, and I continue to wonder whether most people realize how they're behaving.

The 2001 Pixar movie, Monsters Inc, is an animated story about a fictitious world where creatures work to perfect sneaking into children's bedrooms at night and scaring the children to generate energy to fuel their city.[4] This is their job, but the featured monsters eventually learn they can generate more energy by positively affecting these same children through encouragement and laughter than to try and roar their head off, attempting to elicit fear-filled screams.

Obviously, the lovable monsters are from a fictitious animated movie, but the story depicts how these characters realize and adapt to a new way of success. It's not farfetched that we can too.

This is what could happen at our sporting events. A positive-filled, supportive environment with fans pulling for our team and not every contest seemingly a life-or-death matter, would be so much more fulfilling and valuable to our overall well-being. However, excitable fans losing control by crossing the lines of emotion define the current norm.

I remember a successful high school basketball coach who was able to have the privilege of coaching his son. Then I remember seeing that son move on to one of the state's Division I collegiate programs, only to see him drop out of sports after his freshman year because he was burned out.

This young man was from what appeared to be a model family, with no apparent excessive pressure, but the boy had been part of organized sports since he was very young, and he was tired of it. He wasn't having fun anymore. Again, this was from a model family. Think of what it's like for a child with overbearing parents at home and at contests, who expect their child to be the next Michael Jordan or Kobe Bryant or (fill in the name here).

When we develop tense muscles, fast breathing, increased heart rate and constricted blood vessels, we should be experiencing what it means to be an athlete. When these symptoms emerge while we're a fan, we're bucking for headaches, hyperventilation, high blood pressure and ulcers, and maybe taking some of the fun away from others.[5] Remember what the senior official told the father in that youth tournament? The official insisted the father act like an adult, or he would be escorted out of the gym. That gentleman immediately complied, and there were no more issues during that game. Is it that simple? Actually, yes.

Does it make sense for these emotional incidents to happen as fans? The intention of sports is to engage competitively in an activity governed by a set of rules. I think we've got that part down. The purpose of sportsmanship is to display an attitude that strives for fair play, courtesy toward teammates and opponents, ethical behavior, and grace in losing. This is where we need some work.

Are you the fan in the stands getting up and bringing embarrassment to your school community, or are you the one kindly asking the ingrate to *please sit down?* Is your child in the timeout huddle with their head down because they're embarrassed of how you're behaving as a parent in the stands?

As a parent, are you on a sportsmanship committee? Do you help officials find their locker room at contests? Maybe you are a greeter to welcome opposing fans.[6]

If we are adamant in our mission of enforcing great sportsmanship, people will get in line or get out of the way. It's that simple, but we have to truly believe it's the right thing to do. We want that line of leadership to get longer, so it becomes more than a passing fancy – it becomes the new normal.

When COVID-19 statistics trended for the better, health officials were convinced things were improving because people cooperated to help "flatten the curve." People adapted to things they weren't comfortable doing at first but became easier to do because they practiced them for numerous weeks. People who sacrificed and risked during the pandemic were viewed as heroes – beacons of light for others.

The "virus" of crossing the emotional line at sporting events, is something we can cure, too. Being involved in a positive manner is a way of helping a successful athletic event, and it requires quite a few people who are willing to step out and insist on a new way. If we are consistent in enforcing the positive way, we will learn to know where our emotional line is and stay behind it.

In other words, we'll all help flatten the curve of poor sportsmanship, and make the sports world a better place.

Chapter 3

Respect

In a conversation one time with a friend, I was challenged to compare how sportsmanship has evolved over the years. What was it like back then? Is it different now?

To be honest, something is missing today. I remember a genuine respect for the games we played and a reverence for our opponents.

Sure, there were some characters, but mostly I recall classic coaches who appreciated the opportunity before them and taught players to do the same. Before all the viewing opportunities we have today, sports weren't as big and it seemed the focus was on teaching participants how to respectively participate on the fields of play, and in the stands – to be role models – instead of trying to win at all costs, no matter how disrespectful and unsportsmanlike it could get.

A college coach was asked what type of on-field player behavior would not be tolerated by him and his program. "No trash-talking." "No arguing with referees." "No hanging your head after making a mistake, be it a dropped pass or a fumble." "In life," he said, "there are going to be a lot more adverse things than what happens on a football field." "I don't care if we win, lose or draw," he said. "I want them to walk across the field, shake hands with the other team and tell them, 'Good game and good luck.'" This coach made it clear he cared most about how his players acted as they were carrying out their daily lives. This is an example of how I remember most sports coaches and adults acting when I was young and active.

Perhaps surprisingly, this example was Auburn University's Gus Malzahn as he was addressing the crowd at a high school awards luncheon the week before the 2013 SEC Championship game against Missouri. Unfortunately, in today's world, we don't necessarily see Malzahn's approach as the norm, but more like the exception. Because of the pressure to win, coaches are consistently pushing the envelope to get an edge. In the old days, it seemed coaches did whatever they could between games to prepare their teams, so the coaches weren't the ones dictating or micromanaging the outcome of the contest – the players were. Nowadays, football coaches seem like they're on the field more than their players are. Basketball coaches practically run up and down in front of their team bench, expanding the coaches' box until they're told to get back in, and this example is consequently set for the players and the fans in the stands. The pattern I see in today's sports is coaches and players – including parents and fans – continuing to push the limits of the rules until someone has the courage to put them back in their place. There is so much money involved in college and professional sports, and, for some reason, everyone seems to act like they're working to get a piece of it.

Unfortunately, this misbehavior deserves more than a pat, it deserves a veritable whack, and we need to get back to some old-fashioned respect on and off the field – just like the good old days.[7]

Veteran Green Bay Press-Gazette high school beat writer Scott Venci was asked if sportsmanship has improved since he began his sports writing career, and he emphatically stated, "If anything, it's getting worse. Everything now is more heightened. It feels like the stakes are higher for the people involved. Professional salaries keep going up, college tuition keeps going up, and parents think all of their kids are Division I athletes, when they might only be Division III, and there's nothing wrong with that. Putting that kind of pressure on kids can ruin the whole experience for their kids, and then the parents are after the coaches all the time about their kid's playing time." Venci went on to comment how coaches have to worry about setting boundaries for the parents, otherwise so much of their time would be dealing with constant inquiries about why a parent's child isn't playing more. Is respect for these people (yes, coaches are people, too) even being considered in these situations?

Respect is a character trait we can all utilize better. Growing up,

I was always taught to respect my elders and to treat others the way I would like them to treat me (the Golden Rule). When competition kicks in, does that mean we can forego respect for others on the field and in the stands – do whatever it takes to win? No, I am saying we should respect people because it's the right thing to do.

When my boys were younger, I attended one of their games where the competition was intense, and the score was close. Some of the opposition felt the need to talk trash during the game – even to fans in the stands. Based on the behavior of the parents and players, you'd think world peace was going to be determined by the outcome. When observing how parents act, you can understand why some kids behave the way they do. Let's reflect. Because a human being puts on a black-and-white striped shirt, should that change how we treat them? Because a kid puts on a hockey helmet, does that give us the right to berate how they play? Like the next person, I believe in freedom of speech, but I also believe in self-control and common sense. Both need to be practiced before deciding to flap our gums.

When you watch a youth basketball game, and you hear someone complain about every little thing during the game, doesn't it make you wonder if some people lose all sense of reality when they're at a sporting event? I know when I focus on enjoying watching my kids play, I wonder *can anything be better?* When I maintain that focus, I feel much more relaxed and appreciative of the experience we all just went through, and it doesn't matter what the outcome is – even if the opposing team makes a winning shot at the buzzer. Remember, results don't determine our worth – how we respect people and the games we play does. Instead of filling up with pride, we need to fill up with respect – for others – no matter what their role in any sporting event.[8]

There used to be a KFC commercial showing a couple of youth baseball teams facing off. After their contest, both teams walked through the congratulatory line, offering high fives, and demonstrating great sportsmanship. The ad concluded when parents repeated the gesture while carrying buckets of chicken for the post-game picnic. This would be an awesome way for every athletic contest to end and as sweet as harmonic music. Sometimes it seems like a struggle to get there, but showing respect to opponents is a simple, fun gesture we can all do.

Can you imagine every game of major tournaments, like soccer's World Cup, ending with opponents gathering for a chicken dinner? Me neither, but finishing a game with proper etiquette brings closure and balance to a contest. Respect like this isn't only for the so-called traditional sports. It may come in a different shape or form, but it certainly applies to non-traditional sports – like the great outdoors.

When we enter the outdoor sporting world, there are just as many opportunities to display proper sportsmanship – proper respect, and these outings usually involve adults and/or parents of aspiring outdoor enthusiasts. When spending a few spring days in the north woods, no day could start better than seeing a mother bear and her young one off the side of the road. We all know, if the bear family would attempt to cross the busy highway, we'd all stop in our awestruck tracks and watch them cross, right? Can we show sportsmanship to a bear, or to any wild animal? Not in the way we do humans, but we can show respect by obeying the laws of hunting and fishing.

Do we wait for the proper season to start? While hunting, do we wait until the manual's daily start time, or do we take an early shot at the unsuspecting, grazing buck because no one else will know? What example would that set for Johnny or Suzie sitting next to you in your stand? While fishing, do we wait our turn and stay a respectful distance from another boat, even if we're upset because they're in our favorite secret (or so we thought) spot? Whether it's a picnic after a game or watching nature from a distance, respect can generate sweet music, just like the gentle breeze through the evergreens or a serenading wolf in the great outdoors.[9]

When we're sitting in the stands as parents or fans, it's relatively simple for us to be respectful and good sports, because it's all up to the single decision of choosing to stay emotionally under control.

For coaches, it can be more challenging in how they conduct contests where their team has established a sizable margin over their opponent. I respect coaches who are concerned about the well-being of their opponents. This is of utmost importance at the youth level.

How can coaches guard against running up the score? Wisconsin high school football rules contain a built-in control with a running clock that goes into effect during the second half of games in which one team is at least 35 points ahead. Most of the time, the running clock prevents further embarrassment, but sometimes the running clock may not help. In those situations, how can a coach do his best to show respect to opponents?

Besides removing starters from the game and running the ball to take more time, an obscure rule, which most people don't even know about, could be used. Certain levels of football have a rule that allows the team scored upon to decide to kick or receive. After building an insurmountable lead, a coach decided to utilize this rule by kicking off again – instead of receiving – after being scored upon. This gave the other team an additional opportunity to score more points and maintain its dignity. In the days when there was no running clock, this was, and still is, an appropriate way to show respect.

Baseball and softball coaches have the 10-run rule to shorten games, if necessary, but coaches can also put a stop to stealing bases, advancing on passed balls and wild pitches and other situations in which normal advancements would take place.

Basketball and hockey coaches can teach their players to make extra passes when they have a big lead, insisting on only shooting when close to the net or hoop. This not only guards against running up the score but serves as a great self-discipline drill for future close games. Applying the full-court press in basketball when ahead by a wide margin is never acceptable, and those that justify doing it because "that's their only method of play" are offering a weak excuse.

When the integrity of the game and respect for our opponents are kept in the forefront of our minds, decisions to go for it – or not

– should be easier.[10] Parents can do their part in supporting these coaching acts of sportsmanship by knowing the rules, so when they see these sportsmanlike gestures taking place in contests, they'll understand what's taking place instead of simply thinking the coach doesn't know what he/she is doing. Schools could proactively establish preseason sessions for parents and fans to learn the rules of the games they love to support, and during these educational times, it would be a great opportunity for coaches to lead and show their heart and passion for the games they teach. It will also place extra incentive on the coaches to thoroughly know the rules of the game. We generally conclude all coaches already know what's allowed, however, as a former official, it always surprised me how many coaches were not very fluent on the requirements of the game they coached. Therefore, having an orientation for parents and fans would help their program on and off the field of play.

If I sit down to watch television for something other than sporting events, I like to watch certain shows on MeTV. When sitcom wife Suzanne Pleshette asked Bob Newhart one time what he was watching, he responded, "The classics." I love the classics, because I watch them to laugh and remember what seemed to be a simpler time. Arguably, not all shows on MeTV, TV Land or any other similarly-focused stations are classics, but what stands out is how certain life situations played out back in the 1960's or '70s vs. today.

The classic show (at least in my eyes), "Leave it to Beaver" displays a family in which life seemed to run quite smoothly. The major issues for the Cleaver family don't even seem to compare to significant issues of today. One issue that does jump out at me from some of those shows is the lack of respect for authority. In "Adam-12" and "Dragnet," it is amazing how many episodes depicted disrespect towards police officers. However, as demonstrated in the shows, the officers tried to respond in a controlled manner, educating during the process, and usually quickly calming the situation. Sadly, I understand the shows were attempting to reflect the times of when they were created. I just hope history isn't repeating itself, as lack of respect for authority sure seems to be one of the most widespread social problems in society today, especially with our youth. Unfortunately, this disrespect is reinforced through modern-day television programs as well as musical lyrics.

For instance, over the last few years, the situation involving police relations with minorities in communities in our country has been a very touchy subject. If a minority is killed in what is, or appears to be, a racial travesty, protests ring out about racial inequality. The majority of people protest in a peaceful manner; however, a percentage of people resort to violence, including vandalism and looting. There are ways to bring attention to problems, and then there are those who cross the line of emotion and end up getting into trouble in a very different way.

Respect for authority should begin in the home, not taught by the television. This is where our parents need to step up. If kids aren't taught to show respect for their parents, then there's little chance they'll show respect outside the home. We need to teach our children to honor and respect the authorities in their lives, whether it's teachers at school or church, government officials, the police, or coaches and referees.

Respect for authority comes by believing these people are here to help us, not to control or hurt us. This is especially important to teach when we may not agree with decisions from authoritative figures. Should we blindly obey those in authority? No, we shouldn't. Leaders must be held accountable, too. However, we all need to realize that with authority comes responsibility, and there is a proper time and method for responding.

When establishing community youth sports programs, be sure to determine expectations for participants. A community can get a black eye in a hurry if coaches or players of youth sports teams develop a reputation of disrespectfully lashing out at game officials or tournament organizers.

Even volunteers with the best intentions need to be trained and have expectations set for them. This will help them relax and be more respectful in their positions. It also follows that someone must inspect what they expect – i.e., follow through. Set up a structure where volunteers' talents can be utilized to the fullest. Not everyone is meant to be a coach, official, etc. Behind-the-scenes people are needed, too.

Nonetheless, we can all work together better, and teaching others to be respectful is a great place to start.[11]

One approach that helps me is appreciating the little things in life most of us don't have the time to even notice. Is there an opportunity for quiet time in your day? My early-morning walks with my dog are my quiet time, but they have also evolved to be an exciting time of adventure, not only surviving challenging weather in the winter, but drivers who may not see us. On nicer days, enjoying deer in different locations, or watching a great horned owl watch us while perched on the corner fence post of the local tennis courts gets the adrenaline flowing for me, and nothing beats the surprise critter visits. Beware of the ornery raccoon popping out of the woods at a moment's notice, or the mother fox following you because you unknowingly might be getting too close to her den.

As I journey through neighborhoods, I also have witnessed helpful decorative tips for holidays at different times of the year. It's amazing what you'll see or hear if you're looking and/or listening for it. I challenge everyone to leave their ear buds at home and enjoy the wonderful sounds of nature to help us get right with this world.

On one of our journeys, my attention was drawn to an interesting lawn sign that read "Proud Parent of a Navy Sailor Lives Here." At the bottom of the sign were displayed the words "Honor, Courage, Commitment." Those parents are rightfully pleased with what their son or daughter is accomplishing by being part of the Navy. We've also all probably seen the bumper stickers where parents proudly proclaim their children are honor students. Those displays are awesome for the right reasons.

There's one sign I'd like to see when I'm out walking, but I don't think it exists. It would read: "This is the Home of a Family that Practices Good Sportsmanship." As I continue to attend sporting events, and as I've tried to demonstrate in this book, I'm not convinced everyone knows what good sportsmanship looks like, which provides opportunities for those who like to teach.

For instance, at a high school girls' basketball tournament game, the student fans of one school were proclaiming the free throw shooter of the other school had fecal matter in her shorts and then repeated the four-letter word over and over in an attempt to distract the shooter. Because the student section recited this "cheer" in unison, I have no doubt this chant had been used on prior occasions, maybe even throughout the entire season. Disappointingly, this all took place after the pregame sportsmanship expectations were read and established. This also occurred with the school's head administrator in attendance. Nonetheless, the chant didn't come to a stop until a parent from the offended school went and reported it to a host school attendant. It wasn't even the mother of the offended player.

How cool is that?

The host school attendant then went to the student section and instructed them to stop with the offensive chant. He followed that up by reporting the incident to the head administrator who, of course, seemed surprised his students would do such a thing. I know there are proactive schools practicing good sportsmanship and encouraging kids to use their sharp minds to come up with something clean, fun, and encouraging. This school was having fun, but sadly, it was at someone else's expense. The way I understand it, the pregame sportsmanship statement frowns at that.

Once again, those who are supposed to know better did not follow up until someone asked them, and I truly believe if more people have mother-like courage like the parent in this situation, we can get through to our kids that respect is important, and disrespect is unacceptable.[12]

One thing we do a very poor job of doing is respecting the differences in people, but coaches will be the first to admit they look for athletes to fill different roles.

For example, are you the type of person who likes to eat breakfast food for dinner? Truthfully, I don't mind an omelet occasionally, toward the end of the day, or maybe even a skillet of food all "thrown" together at one of the local family restaurants. Sometimes, these meals may not be prepared exactly the way we like them. How do we react when that happens?

What happens if you're a coach and not every player on your team is a bonafide star? The situations are similar.

One of the breakfast items easily ruined is toast. Here is a story passed on to me about burnt toast.

There was this little girl whose mom liked to make breakfast food for dinner every so often. One night in particular, the mother made breakfast food after a long, grinding day at work. That evening, the mother placed a helping of eggs, sausage and extremely burned toast in front of the little girl's dad. The girl remembered waiting to see if anyone would say something about the condition of the toast. The father didn't hesitate, but reached for his toast, smiled at the girl's mother, and asked the girl how her day was at school. The girl couldn't remember what she told him, but she did remember watching him smear butter and jelly on that toast and eat every bite.

When she got up from the table that evening, she remembered hearing her mom apologize to her dad for burning the toast – for making an apparent mistake. Without blinking an eye, he told her he loved burned toast.

Later that night, when the girl went to kiss her dad goodnight, she asked him if he really liked his toast burned. He wrapped his daughter in his arms and said, "Your mom put in a hard day at work today, and she's really tired. A little burnt toast never hurt anyone."

Life is full of imperfect things and imperfect people. Just look in the mirror, to find the nearest example. The majority of us aren't the best cooks or housekeepers. We may not be the best coach or referee. What we need to do is learn to accept each other's faults – choosing to celebrate each other's differences. This is one of the most important keys to creating healthy, growing, lasting, and respectful relationships.

Learn to take the good, the bad and the ugly parts of your life and make the best of them. Burnt toast (our differences) should never break up a relationship. This display of respect can be applied to all relationships – as understanding is the basis of any relationship, be it a husband-wife, parent-child, friendship, coach-parent, or coach-player. As the old saying goes, "Don't put the key to your happiness in someone else's pocket – keep it in your own."

In the meantime, let's all learn to enjoy some burnt toast.[13]

The bottom line is we can do better in respecting others, and our world will be a better place when we get to that point!

Chapter 4

Follow-up and Follow-through

As I mentioned earlier, my dad was an only child raised on a small, modest farm in rural Wisconsin. As he described it one time, he was a kid whose close friends were the animals he took care of. So, because of limited interaction with others, one might think he'd be someone who wouldn't have developed any interpersonal relationship skills. However, it was specifically how he handled himself with others, especially those who visited Grandma and Grandpa on the farm, that indirectly taught me how to interact respectfully. I was fortunate to witness those exchanges while we were at the farm to help with chores like cutting the lawn, picking fruit, chopping wood, or fixing fences. One distinct memory exists regarding the fact Sundays were usually meant for recharging for the upcoming week, or by visiting others. As a whole, that certainly isn't the case anymore.

His father was educated through the sixth grade, and from my recollection, always seemed to be a gruff, crotchety old man. Because of that, we didn't get close to him, and before I had a chance to really get to know him, he passed away when I was fifteen. During his life, Grandpa was dedicated to his farm and was convinced he needed my dad to help him on a full-time basis. Therefore, if it wasn't for my grandmother, a teacher by trade, my dad would have only been able to attend school through the sixth grade, too. Dad was also smart, succeeding as a civil engineer without the benefit of a college education. Most impressive to me was his ability to fix just about anything. I'm sure his farm days helped with that, but nonetheless, my dad's humble beginnings and abilities became more apparent and understood as I grew up. I believe it helped me respect all he did for us, and ultimately appreciate everything he provided us in life.

Nonetheless, Grandma's efforts and encouragement enabled my dad to have the privilege to attend *and* graduate from high school. This opportunity allowed Dad to be exposed to sports, which led to the blessing of participating in one year of organized track and field. I will be eternally grateful for Grandma's support because it allowed my dad enough of an exposure to one particular coach, who helped Dad develop a love for sports, which he passed on to me.

Dad's sports experiences were obviously limited, but I never would have guessed that based on his efforts on our behalf. His awareness and patience were evident on a daily basis. He seemed to know the nuances of my favorite sports, even though he didn't have the opportunity to really learn and practice those pastimes. He and/or Mom were at every event we had, in a positively supporting way. One thing for certain, I never had to worry about Mom or Dad embarrassing us by yelling at the officials, coaches, or me.

One of my favorites, if not *the* favorite sport was basketball, probably because of my beginnings back in the garage. The first year I could participate in an organized league, sponsored by the local YMCA, was fifth grade. My very first coaches were Dad and my older cousin. We had some exciting games while wearing our custom silk-screened Supersonic T-shirts that my cousin designed and created. It was such a comfort for me to have my dad working in tandem with my cousin and providing a welcoming environment in my first year of organized sports.

One of the things Dad emphasized right from the beginning was the importance of free-throw shooting, because he was convinced games were more often determined by one or two points. His clear message was whichever team shot free throws better, more than likely won most of its games.

Certainly, there are many ways to shoot a foul shot, but success will be limited without a proper follow-through.

Former NBA star Karl Malone was quite deliberate before shooting the ball as he seemingly talked to himself. Adrian Dantley appeared to massage the ball before releasing, Rick Barry shot underhand and Wilt Chamberlain appeared to try to put the ball through the backboard instead of the rim while standing about two feet behind the free throw line. Percentage-wise, Rick Barry was the most successful shooter from the list above, but none of their styles mattered when they didn't follow through.

The same needs to apply in sportsmanship.

Before high school basketball games in my home state of Wisconsin, it is often announced that good sportsmanship is required by the host school, its conference, and the Wisconsin Interscholastic Athletic Association.

Like styles of free throws, this verbiage probably varies from school to school and state to state, but it's communicated to us that sportsmanship is important and is demonstrated by respecting and positively supporting players, coaches, fans, and officials. Some schools also go on to remind adults, especially parents, they are the most important example for the student body.

I have no problems with that requirement. A requirement is a demand and sets our expectations as parents. This is all well and good, unless we fail to follow through.

Allowing kids to stand the entire game is fine, until they personally call out to an opposing player preparing at the foul line. Even if the kids are sitting, but confronting players from the other team, we are failing to follow through. The same goes for parents.[14]

Honestly, there are too few times I can remember when I've attended an athletic contest at which the host school has followed through on the promise of enforcing this requirement. The times I have seen or heard it enforced has been at events where objectionable behavior clearly took place, and after something was done, by either the school administrator or a contest official, the rest of the event went off without a hitch.

If we're unwilling to confront unacceptable behavior, does it make sense to read a code of expectations at the beginning of athletic contests?

Simple follow-throughs could consist of an athletic director/contest manager going up into the stands and issuing a warning to an unruly parent. However, experience has shown simple warnings usually aren't the definitive answer. Quite often, the solution comes down to asking an unruly parent or fan to leave the contest. Yes, it takes courage to do this, but it'll be easier the more consistently it's done. Eventually, word will get out, and parents will have it in their head to behave or face the consequences of being asked to leave. This will set expectations for parents as well as anyone else in the gym.

Ejections could be eliminated if parents would hold each other accountable, by calling out violators and getting them to stop their problematic behavior before it gets out of control. It may even mean a school administrator won't have to take action.

I truly believe the follow-up on poor sportsmanship isn't as difficult as we make it out to be except when it's put off until "next time" in perpetuity.

Ryan Borowicz, owner of The Driveway, a basketball training center in the Green Bay (Wisconsin) area, is convinced we need someone to take a stance in different sports situations, so we can do the right thing from a sportsmanship standpoint every time. Borowicz, a former Division I basketball player at University of Wisconsin-Green Bay, believes if parents are out of line, we need to say something to them every time, especially if they are from their own team. "We're not going to wait for the tournament director to kick them out," said Borowicz. Just like at his basketball facility, the expectations are set with kids from Day 1, in that they're not going to be allowed to goof off, and if a kid does, proper follow-through will take place. The same process can work with parents.

What could follow-up look like if a coach followed through on what he perceived was either unsportsmanlike acts or lack of character by his team?

Here is a story to demonstrate how a high school coach in Utah was disturbed enough by his players' off-the-field behavior that he took action. On the surface, we shouldn't be pleased when inappropriate behavior takes place, but it was the coach's follow-through that made me smile.

Instead of making his team perform extra wind sprints or push-ups, this coach suspended the entire 80-member team after a

Friday night loss. Remember, it wasn't their on-the-field results that bothered the coach. It was the off-the-field antics, which included skipping class, disrespecting teachers, and cyberbullying.

The coach felt he needed to make a stand. After the game, he made them all turn in their uniforms and equipment. He then told the players they would all have to earn the privilege to play again.

You see, this is what most people forget. It is a *privilege* to play for your high school team – not a right. No one is entitled to play high school sports – no matter how much offseason money is spent. The same can be said for attending sporting events. No one has the right to be there. It is a privilege, and it can, and should, be taken away if people, especially parents, don't fulfill their role at a sporting event.

In the story, the coaching staff announced a 7 a.m. meeting for the next morning when all the interested kids would get a chance to earn back their spots on the team. At the meeting, the coach handed out a letter to each of his players and made it very clear what needed to happen to rejoin.

The following week's scheduled game was not cancelled, but the Union High School football team from Roosevelt, Utah did not practice all week. Instead, the team performed community service, went to study hall and attended a class on character development. The "final exam" was a self-reflective report as to why the coach's displeasure was justified.

There's a very strong chance the life lesson will never be forgotten by those players. The time and effort spent on taking a step backward by the program, actually vaulted it forward.

I wish more coaches and administrators would demonstrate their knowledge of how valuable sports can be for this teaching of life's lessons. Sometimes teams and/or individuals need to lose before they can learn how to win – on or off the field of play.

When inappropriate behaviors surface at sporting events in the adult/parent section of the stands, hopefully someone will maturely step forward at the right time to take advantage of the teachable moment – just like the coach in Utah.[15]

The exercise taught those players a great lesson. I believe the same thing can happen if parents are similarly taught. Perhaps the reason parents continue to violate sportsmanship in an unacceptable fashion is because very few are willing to step forward and help them learn the very lesson the aforementioned football players experienced and are better human beings because of it.

Longtime youth football coach and team President of the Allouez (Wisconsin) Buccaneers, Paul Ihlenfeldt relayed an example of how a parent can be similarly taught, when he recalled a father and son combination no one in town wanted to be part of any team or program. In reality, no one wanted the son to play on their team because of the father, and his poor reputation. As Ihlenfeldt described it, "The father was a big mouth, who wouldn't shut-up, and created problems." Ihlenfeldt went on to tell the father he was pretty sure their program was his last chance, that he wanted to help them for his son, and that the father needed to behave. The father was guaranteed if he didn't behave, he wouldn't be allowed to attend games or practices. If that came to pass, and then the father couldn't stay away from games and practices, then the father *and* his son would be removed from the team and the program altogether. As Ihlenfeldt communicated, because of the way he set expectations and followed through, the father and son were able to make it through the whole season.

Here is a similar follow-through lesson that came to me at an early age and has helped me relate to sportsmanship.

When I was in elementary school, during the days before today's technological advances and receiving computer printouts of teacher assignments and class schedules, we didn't find out who our new teacher was going to be until the first day of school when we read the class list above the door. In fourth grade, there was great concern among my friends and me about the possibility of getting one particular teacher who had a terrible reputation for being very strict. We walked from classroom to classroom trying to find our names, and class by class, I discovered my name wasn't on the lists of the teachers I had hoped to get. As I approached the last room, it was all but a matter of procedure to look up and feel my heart sink when seeing my name on her class list.

As the school year progressed, I realized I had overreacted. She turned out to be a pretty good teacher who simply expected a lot from her students. For instance, one day she made one of my classmates wash his hands over four times until the cleanliness met her expectations. She also was bound and determined to make sure we eliminated a particular improper usage of grammar when we would say, "My mother, she..." or "My friend, he...".

To this day, the value of cleanliness, proper language, and some of her other fundamental teachings still resonate with me. Why? Because she followed-up and followed-through.

When I began the eighth grade, I found out our school had a brand-new English and Social Studies teacher. I'd say when a new teacher arrives, there aren't any preconceived notions, right? She seemed nice enough when she was introduced to the junior high student body, but I found out later in class, she was a tough newcomer with high standards. Being a good student, it wasn't that I minded the high standards. She just seemed a bit too curt for our liking, and I quickly found out what that looked like. In an early school-year project, I was a bit careless and comical in preparing my illustrations to support a written paper, and she let me know it in her comments. I wasn't happy with that particular project's grade, but that was the only warning I needed to adjust quickly and never experience that embarrassment again.

Both teachers had reputations or gave impressions of holding unrealistic standards, but once getting to know them and understanding what they were all about, it was a joy to be in their classrooms and to be part of those expectations.

Obviously, everyone had a different personality and approach to school, so not everyone benefited from those teachers the way I did. Those teachers had high expectations of us as students, and I believe those high expectations should be expected of parents and other participants at sporting events, too.

I also believe high expectations should be demanded when it comes to sportsmanship.

Expectations were set early in the school year, and then they were followed up on by our teachers. As the school year progressed and we met those expectations, there were times when our teachers relaxed some of those requirements. However, as soon as we took things too far, we were brought back into line with discipline and consequences.

It's no different when walking our dog. If he behaves, I'm more willing to give him extra leash. However, when he gets out of control, I have to shorten the leash and get back to basics.

It all seems so easy.

That's where I wish those who conduct sporting events would truly establish boundaries for fan behavior that are only considered successful when accompanied with proper follow-through. If reading the sportsmanship statement is setting the expectations, then the follow-up when fans misbehave must be included. As students, we appreciated when our teachers were consistent. As fans, we appreciate when officials are, too. I've got a feeling all other sports participants will appreciate the day when fans, especially parents, fall in line with their consistency also.[16]

Chapter 5

Patience

When pursuing jobs throughout my career, I'd try to anticipate what interview questions would be asked, and how I *should* answer them. After college, we have little knowledge in how to prepare for this experience. Even if your school offered soft skills training in what to expect when looking for a job, that theoretical practice helped, but doesn't account for every scenario. Honestly, Marquette University provided help to interested students, but I didn't take advantage of it. Therefore, I naively went into the interviewing process and learned how to better interview by failing as I went along. Certainly, I could have done more research to prepare for the process, but no matter how much studying is done, there will always be questions that you don't expect.

One of the common challenges I faced wasn't even a question, but more of a request; to identify my strengths and weaknesses. Some potential employers wanted me to name five of each. Because I was fresh out of college, I was confident, so identifying what I thought were strengths was easier for me than listing my weaknesses. I'm not sure how much self-reflecting I'd done to that point in my life, but nonetheless, I was more interested in focusing on my strengths. I don't remember ever filling up the five-lines of weaknesses in organizations that wanted that many. From my perspective, it seemed almost like a lose-lose proposition. If I identified that many weaknesses, why would they want to hire someone with that many faults? You could also look at it in the way that if I had five glaring faults, I wasn't being very confident in myself. From the other end of the spectrum, you could say the identification of five weaknesses demonstrated a true transparent and honest candidate. Who knows? I could have missed the whole psychological boat behind that entire exercise, but the important point is that it hasn't hurt me in the end.

When it came down to actually identifying weaknesses, I was able to conclude patience was my greatest. I doubt I was the only college graduate to claim that.

Patience was something I have always had a challenge with, but as far as my job hunt out of college, I was hoping one interview would be all I needed to kick-start my career. Nonetheless, I was forced to practice patience through the job-search process. Because the first interview didn't immediately lead to my first job, and I wasn't one of those fortunate/well-prepared college seniors who had a job waiting for them after graduation. I would have to be patient and persistent moving forward.

Fresh out of college, it was difficult knowing what I wanted to do, especially since I had challenges deciding on a path of study to begin with. Switching my major halfway through school, and fearful I was going to be on the "ten-year plan," I simply wanted to graduate and move forward in life.

Because I was still living at home, and had the comfort of knowing Mom and Dad weren't going to charge me rent, I didn't need to rush into anything just in the name of taking a job, right? I loved the idea of coaching high school basketball, but would that be considered a real job? In those days, intentional, or not, it was made clear in order to be successful, I needed to pursue a financially rewarding career. Besides, I was voted most likely to succeed in my graduating class.

It seemed most high school coaches in those days were also teachers, who I felt didn't make enough money. I also had not pursued a teaching degree and thought my hopes of coaching were done.

I wanted to do something our Creator wanted me to do, but that choice isn't always going to be clearly delivered on a silver platter, either. My inexperience had me torn as to whether I needed to wait for developments or plow forward. When I thought I should be moving forward, I had feelings of being on the craziest path possible in trying to reach my goal of getting a job. I was struggling with when to be patient and when to be stepping out in faith. Don't all young people experience this?

I should have realized it wouldn't be easy, because when you pursue something worthwhile, it takes time, and that's where the patience factor comes in. In fact, I should have known better because of the lesson I learned the very first day my dad introduced me to patience.

When I was about eight years old, my father took my brother and me fishing on a small, quiet lake, perfect for canoes or row-boats; motorboats weren't allowed.

It was early in the morning as we quietly paddled our canoe to what Dad thought would be a good spot. This was one of his favorite lakes for fishing, and as I reflect, I can now understand why. Overall, it was very peaceful, even though it was loaded with nature. I remember the woodpeckers banging away on trees, red-winged blackbirds serenading us from the cattails, snapping turtles splashing from their fallen logs and bullfrogs croaking to their hearts' delight. Critters galore set the scene for a wonderful morning of fishing.

Dad liked the lake so much, he had brought us there before as a family for swimming, canoeing and a picnic, but I didn't notice then what I noticed on this particular morning. Unbeknownst to me, this was going to be the day when I learned a valuable lesson in patience.

We hear about athletes who demonstrate patience as they wait for a hole to open in football, or as a shot develops in basketball. It seemed like patience in the wild was something I could never develop because the results seemed to take so much longer. As adult drivers, do we notice how much longer it seems to take to go somewhere when we've never been there before?

When anglers go fishing, they typically have an anchor they let down to the water's bottom to hold a boat in a desired spot. We did not have one that could reach the depths of this part of the lake, so we were expected to sit quietly as Dad gently maneuvered our canoe to keep us in the same general area while we waited for a fish to bite from somewhere near the bottom. We weren't fishing for surface-dwellers like bluegills. Dad said we were trolling for rainbow trout, a fish that liked to live in the deeper, cooler water. That day, we were being taught how to catch a more challenging and elusive fish, and it required some additional skills.

John Quincy Adams once quoted, "Patience and perseverance have a magical effect before which difficulties disappear and obstacles vanish."

In the past, my experiences at this lake had amounted to fun through immediate gratification. Now I was expected to wait for the prize of the catch. I was being taught joy can come in the form of waiting, as in enjoying the journey. It was different from what I had known, and it was difficult. However, I now believe most sports enthusiasts can do a better job of enjoying the journey. Unfortunately, too many people want quick satisfaction by getting right to the prize. Heck, getting five hamburgers from a McDonald's drive-through only takes a few minutes.

As a rookie, I wasn't the most patient student that day. In my limited fishing experiences, I was accustomed to casting my line into the water from a pier and immediately reeling it in, hoping a fish would jump at the very sight of a big, fat nightcrawler. That certainly wasn't a realistic approach for this day's adventure.

Trolling and sitting was different, and I was having a hard time being convinced I wanted any future part of it. Besides, aluminum canoes aren't the quietest devices when young boys are shifting in their seat or on the bottom of the canoe, and accidentally kicking the sides.

Every few minutes we prodded our dad to give us permission to crank in our line and see if something had taken our bait or begged him to move to a new spot. He kept reminding us we needed to have more self-control, which led me to conclude patience was beginning to become an unsightly word.

After what seemed an eternity, we paddled the canoe to the point of this lake that looked like a horseshoe, closer to the landing, and he let us bring in our lines. Sure enough! As I reeled in the slack, I could tell there was something tugging on the other end. By no means would I consider myself a veteran angler, but if you've ever gone fishing, the feeling of a live one on the end of your line is quite exhilarating. It's the goal of going in the first place, right? As it turned out, a rainbow trout, like Dad had earlier described, had taken my bait. We netted it, took a picture, and then set it free.

Dad continued to the landing, but now our "patience" had been rewarded and we had tasted success. Author William Faulkner once wrote, "And sure enough, even waiting will end...if you can just wait long enough." Needless to say, we now wanted to go back and do it all over again.[17]

In a discussion with Robert Brooks, team chaplain of the NFL's Cleveland Browns, Brooks stated, "The only time we have disappointment is when we have unmet expectations, and unmet expectations *usually* come from not being patient. When we are impatient, we find out things we thought would satisfy us, in reality do *not* satisfy us."

The lessons of that day live with me now. For a couple of boys full of vim and vigor, we simply thought we were learning how to fish, and it would be non-stop action. However, in retrospect, our dad was teaching us the gift of being able to calm ourselves through self-control, humility, and delayed gratification, and how to use those assets to work towards a goal.[18] It's a moment of a lifetime for a young sportsman to spend time with his brother and father, to develop a memory that'll last forever.

Obviously, the time spent fishing was quality time with my dad, and people often say Americans need to spend more quality time with their kids. However, time together is what we have control of creating, and the quality aspect of it may, or may not follow. The best part is that my father cared enough to spend time with us and teach the lessons we experienced that morning. Retrospectively, the residual benefit is that those lessons were – and still are – transferable to other sports, family matters, business, etc. It would be fun to rehash that wonderful experience of quality time with my late father.

According to mindful.org there are 4 benefits of patience:

- Patient people enjoy better mental health. By better coping with stressful situations, patient people tend to experience less depression and negative emotion.
- Patient people are better friends and neighbors. In relationships with others, patience becomes a form of kindness.
- Patience helps us achieve our goals. The road to achievement is a long one, and those without patience – who want immediate results – may not be willing to walk it.
- Patience is linked to good health. If patience can reduce daily stress, it can also protect us against the effects of stress.[19]

In youth sports today, it seems to me the prominent impatient party has flipped roles from my fishing story. Back then, the kids were impatient, and the parents were the patient teachers. Now, the parents are the ones who quite often are more impatient, not necessarily the kids, who seem better at going with the flow. Because our world has adopted what's commonly referred to as a "fast food mentality," there is little time for tolerance – especially with parents. Many are impatient with coaches because their kids don't play enough and/or win enough. Parents' restlessness reigns supreme against officials, because invariably every call is a bad one when called against their team. Likewise, based on my first-hand observations, parents certainly don't have peace with their kids, who aren't perfect. With every mistake, the proverbial athletic scholarship guaranteeing a free ride to college seems to slip further away.

Ever since sixth grade, when my future father-in-law was my youth football coach, I had learned to call my own plays as the team's quarterback. Because we never used game film at the youth level to study our opponent, my father-in-law's approach was a little different than my varsity coach's methodology, but they both accomplished the same thing. Our intent was to determine the weaknesses of our opponent and then capitalize on them. On our youth team, it wasn't something we were going to find out in one play, or probably even one series of downs – it was discovered more by experiment. At the varsity level, it was something requiring everyone's input. In essence, we conducted a veritable board meeting between each play, talking about who could beat the opponent across from them, what their opponents were doing, and in twenty-five seconds (the length of the play clock), or less, we needed to summarize the information we had gathered, and come up with a strategy to defeat the team we were playing. It needed to be quick and decisive, and we needed consensus from everyone on the field.

These types of processes take time to develop and learn. Our coach's job was to teach us how to be the best we could be at doing it. He had to have patience in us learning it, but then after a reasonable amount of time, discernment to see if we were the group that could effectively execute his offensive game plan.

Nowadays, football coaches call most plays on offense and defense. Sometimes coaches give permission for the quarterback or defensive captain to call an audible to another play based on what the opponent presented on that set. Generally though, coaches call the plays, and have taken away the opportunity for the board meetings of years ago to take place in the huddle. There is still a need for leadership in all sports, but micromanaging has been inserted into competitions and the opportunities for fulfillment are different.

A few years ago, I spoke with a former NFL Defensive Player of the Year turned high school head football coach who also called his team's defensive plays. I knew he had been calling the defensive signals for some time, so I asked him if he thought players of the day weren't able to handle calling their own plays as they had years ago. His answer came as no surprise to me. He responded that he felt the players of the day were just as capable as players from years ago, but he wasn't allowed the luxury of having patience with his leaders because of parents. You see, if he didn't establish a winning program as soon as possible, because, in part, he was deciding to be patient as his players were learning how to call plays, the parents would complain to the school administration and pressure them to find a new head coach. He said he was interested in being a long-term coach and had to do what he felt he needed to do to stay employed.

This micromanaging, due to lack of time for patience, has seeped into other sports, too. For instance, baseball pitching coaches and managers often decide what kind of pitch should be thrown every time to the batter. Have you noticed how the catchers regularly look into the dugout? They're looking for what pitch they should call this time. I could see this happening occasionally during a game as a suggestion. When I pitched in high school or for adult amateur teams, I relished working with the catcher and strategizing how we were going to try and get certain hitters out. For me, it was a little like baseball's version of the football huddle where the athletes were taught to work together on the field and pursue success without the constant intervention of the coaches on every play or pitch. It was awesome when the catcher and I were aligned in our thinking, and I rarely disagreed in deference to another pitch. As we became used to each other, we became better at thinking the same way, and it created an awesome satisfaction for that aspect of the game that players today don't experience. Because those opportunities and feelings generally have been taken away, you could argue athletes in essence have become more robotic, simply carrying out what they've been ordered to do by coaches. It takes away opportunities to be thinkers on our feet during the heat of action.

Unfortunately, professional sports governing bodies continue to tinker with the rules of our favorite sports. They tell us it's to improve the games we love, when I believe their real intent is to figure out how to make their big business even more lucrative. Subsequently, what is often implemented in the form of rules changes at the professional level eventually makes its way to youth sports in some form or fashion.

One of those items, the unending compulsion to speed up games prevails, instead of reverting to ways where more patience might be involved. As I said, I believe it takes away from the purity of the games we learned as kids, in the name of making more money. I preferred when Hall of Fame Major Leaguer Ernie Banks was hailed as a true sports fanatic, when he proclaimed it was always better to play two games instead of one.

Ultimately, many parents want their kids to be stars of tomorrow. They believe their children have a better chance of drawing attention for scholarships through successful programs. If the children aren't fortunate enough to receive a scholarship, parents have been known to feel it is a reflection on them, and, in turn, they've blamed coaches for not doing enough to help their child. In this scenario, the complaint would be because the coach displayed too much patience in the all-around development of his players.

Another party that receives blame from parents for not doing enough to help their child(ren) is sportswriters. Scott Venci informed me it was a running joke amongst him and his colleagues how all of them early in their careers, at one time or another, were going to be accused by parents of costing their child(ren) a scholarship by not writing about them enough, because parents believe sportswriters have great influence.

What we all need to do is take a deep breath and enjoy the moment we've been given with the games we were taught – even if it is a long one. Life passes us by so quickly anyway. Why do we continually want to speed it up?

Thinking back to my fishing experience, I didn't think patience would ever be something I could list as a strength, but it sure is a good one to list if you can.

Chapter 6

Letting Kids Make Mistakes

One of the greatest mistakes parents can make is to try to prevent their children from making mistakes. It sounds redundant, but when you think about it, it makes sense. This error in judgment comes with a loving heart, as most parents work to help their children have a better life than they did. Unfortunately, putting that protective bubble around our kids actually hinders their progress. It's similar to the story of the caterpillar turning into a butterfly.

Stories are a great way to teach a lesson. This story about a butterfly "fluttered" across my path and is a great illustration of the value of overcoming adversity.

A man found the cocoon of a butterfly. After some time passed, a small opening appeared at the end of the cocoon. The man anxiously sat and watched as the butterfly struggled to force its body through the opening at the end of the cocoon. It seemed like hours. Suddenly, the butterfly seemed halted in its progress. It seemed as if it hit a dead end and could go no farther.

Like any good-natured person would, the man decided to help the butterfly. He took a pair of scissors and snipped off the remaining bit of the cocoon, allowing the butterfly to come out easily. The man continued to watch the butterfly because he anxiously expected to see the wings enlarge and expand to support the body, which would eventually contract.

He pictured how the beautifully marked butterfly would look and fly around the garden because of his help. Neither of those things happened. Just the opposite occurred. The butterfly spent the rest of its life grounded with a swollen body and shriveled wings. It never could fly.

Through his attempt at kindness, the man didn't understand

the challenges presented by the cocoon and the struggle required for the butterfly to get through the tiny opening. This was nature's way of forcing fluid from the body of the butterfly into its wings to prepare for flight once it had worked its way out of the cocoon.

Struggles can be awesome teachers and are sometimes exactly what we need in our life. If we were allowed to travel on our life journey without any obstacles, as with the butterfly, it would hamper us tremendously. We would never reach our true potential. "Flying" would be an impossibility.

Struggles sometimes show us alternatives, but the difficult part is for parents to let go.[20] Why? We want to see our kids succeed. However, in sports and in life, we often see parents making more of a mess, instead of stepping aside and letting children affect their own future. We'll never know until we give them room, but there are times our children might actually do better without our help.

Nowadays, social media can be the home for gossip and cowardly ill-regard for others, but it also can be very good, just like the internet itself. I was forwarded a Facebook post that's in the form of a letter from a father to his young wrestler. I believe this letter could be concerning any sport, because the life lessons of sports are awesome. Unfortunately, too many times we fail to let the kids encounter the total experience. Sometimes, we try to live vicariously through our kids, and prevent them from making mistakes, or experience losing. Honestly, I doubt if there is any parent who truly wants to see their child fail. However, it's okay. Losing teaches great lessons. Here's that wonderful letter:

"You had a tough time on the mat today and the ride home was pretty quiet. I admit I was very disappointed, but I later came to realize I shouldn't be, and it is all part of the journey you are taking. When I watch you on the mat, I worry you are doing battle while unprepared and I have failed in your preparation. As a father, that is my greatest fear – you are unprepared to face the challenges that will come before you. I want you to be prepared for your match, but I've come to realize it is the matches themselves that are, in the long run, win or lose, the things that ARE preparing you.

I think the greatest benefit from wrestling is learning to face challenges and to demand the most from yourself. You learn to fight when you think there is no more fight left within you. You learn to get up after you've fallen, time and time again. You learn about sacrifice and about pain. You learn to endure and to overcome. This is what I want for you, not because I wrestled, but because these lessons are the true gifts of this sport. So, those losses today were actually part of this gift, and an important part of the journey.

My dream for you is not just win championships and fill your room with medals. My dream for you is much greater and I hope you get much more from wrestling. I hope you learn to strive for greatness even if you fail in the attempt. I hope you learn to get up one more time when you think you can't get up any longer. I hope you learn to not only face your fears, but to stare them down.

Wrestling isn't about winning. It is about the desire to win. It isn't about success, but rather the determination to succeed. I want you to succeed as a wrestler, not to win state championships, but I want you to be a successful wrestler so you learn to be all that you can. This sport can help teach you that if you let it. I look forward to the seasons of our future as you go through these lessons, and I'll be in your corner for each and every one of them. I love you. Dad."[21]

Over the years, much has been written about how Tiger Woods' dad handled his son when he was a child. Earl Woods was a longtime member of the U.S. Navy, and reportedly applied his military knowledge to Tiger's golf training routine as a youngster to help Tiger experience stress while he learned the game of golf that would help him when he became a professional. This isn't a training method I'd recommend for having fun, but Tiger Woods has experienced tremendous success as a golfer, and my handicap has plenty of room for improvement.

Ryan Borowicz admits there is a general hesitancy for parents to let kids figure things out on their own when they compete in sports. One way he advocates for kids' creativity is to conduct

3-on-3 basketball leagues at his facility. For these tournaments, he does not allow *any* coaching by parents. I have a hard time imagining the father I mentioned earlier at the Gus Macker Tournament being able to sit down and let his son's team navigate their own games at that time. Borowicz confirmed parents struggle with this rule of his, but, as he stated, "Parents have to realize that most of these kids aren't training to make it to the NBA, but instead they're preparing for what to do when they lose, or how to handle not being a starter anymore. Parents have to realize these are opportunities to learn, to communicate, to talk." Borowicz wishes parents would learn to wait until after the games are completed to "coach" their kids, instead of always wanting to advise them as things are playing out, and then do it in a supportive, loving manner. This penchant for always being involved thwarts our kid's creativity. Borowicz reflected how he and his friends used to play home-run derby when they were kids, without any parental involvement, which encouraged creativity and spontaneity. These are wonderfully learned traits that benefit kids later in life.

Years ago, former professional tennis player Mary Pierce needed a permanent separation from her father because he was not only overbearing, but abusive, too.

Here are some helpful hints provided by Life Skills International (www.lifeskillsintl.org), which may make letting go a bit easier:

- To let go does not mean to stop caring – it means we can't do it for someone else.
- To let go is not to enable, but to allow learning from natural consequences.
- To let go is not to change or blame another, but to make the most of ourselves.
- To let go is not to fix, but to be supportive.
- To let go is not to judge, but to allow another to be a human being.
- To let go is not to be in the middle arranging all the outcomes, but to allow others to affect their own future.

- To let go is not to be protective, but to permit another to face reality.
- To let go is to fear less and love more.[22]

My parents weren't perfect by any means, but there were certain things they felt were important for us to learn. One of the checklist items they wanted us to experience was music lessons. Mom and Dad both loved music, but they never had the opportunity to experience private lessons themselves. Therefore, they were trying to help our lives be better by giving us the opportunity to learn.

I started taking piano lessons when I was in second grade. Obviously, seven years old is a tough age to sit for extended periods. At first, it was difficult for me to understand why I needed to practice, and when I did sit down to play, thirty minutes of practice seemed like forever. Nonetheless, Mom and Dad were trying to help me better myself by pursuing something challenging and new. They didn't force me to take piano lessons, but they knew the value of music in one's life. Therefore, they encouraged me to try it for a year.

What helped indirectly encourage me was to see my father regularly sing in the church choir, or as a soloist at weddings, funerals, or the like. He was good at it, and just watching him encouraged me to keep trying as a piano player. The one thing they never did, as we see too often in athletics, is stay at music lessons and watch over my shoulder, correcting me on every note. In addition, as a beginner, I'm sure what I was producing wasn't really melodic and attractive to the ears, but they were always encouraging. I was surrounded by an environment where making mistakes was okay, as long as I continued to try. That provided a valuable foundation.

My first piano teacher was a well-respected instructor, who had many students. She never married and lived with her sister. Both were music teachers and certainly dedicated to their craft. At any time of the day, you could hear music in that house emanate from the upstairs and downstairs.

My teacher started out by exposing me to fun songs and pieces, and church hymns so I would enjoy myself and want to come back.

My lessons were also thirty minutes, starting at 6:30 a.m. on Saturday mornings, so we could have the rest of the week for other activities. My sister, brother, and I all had our lessons back-to-back-to-back. The town where she lived was about twenty minutes away, so it was easiest to have everyone's lesson take place on one trip. As I progressed, I was being assigned more difficult music, and it was still fun, but I wasn't convinced I had what it took to be a good piano player.

Then she started to enter us into competitions where we would be judged and critiqued on how we played. For musicians at that age, the judging was more about simple suggestions and encouragement, to help us enjoy music. The judging wasn't very faultfinding, nor did it involve competition against others, like would come later during high school. It made me think, did I really want to be judged for every piece of music I played? That seemed like a lot of constructive feedback, and not the most fun.

Then one Saturday morning, everything changed. During my lesson, she asked me to get up from my seat, so she could get something from inside her piano bench. She shuffled through some old newspapers, and then pulled some story clippings of a major league baseball player, who turned out to be her cousin. I loved baseball, and we must have been talking about the recreation team I played on. At first, I didn't think much of the clippings she showed me, until she pointed out a player I recognized, someone everyone would recognize. It was Babe Ruth from the New York Yankees! Then she pointed to her cousin standing next to Babe Ruth in the picture. Holy cow! Her cousin knew Babe Ruth, arguably the most famous baseball player of all time. As it turned out, her cousin was famous in his own right, not only as a Major League Baseball player, but because he was the owner of a unique record all to himself. Her cousin was Bill Wambsganss, who, to this day, is the only player to have ever recorded an unassisted triple play in World Series history. When second baseman Wambsganss, moving to his right, caught a line shot, he was able to step on second base to double off the runner who had been on second, and then tag the runner coming from first who hadn't been able to adjust to the sharply hit ball. Suddenly, my piano teacher's cousin was the owner of a record that is now one hundred years old. How cool is that?

When my piano teacher brought this to my attention, she was demonstrating to me how she wanted to connect with me through interests of mine. I now realize I was in the company of a woman who was going to teach me more than just how to play in a recital. She was also going to teach me about life, and that my value wasn't determined by how I tickled the ivory. That day, she transformed from being my piano "coach", and turned into my friend. As it turned out, the six years I had with her were a lot of fun learning to play Beethoven and Chopin, Queen and Scott Joplin, to name only a handful of the composers she exposed me to. Because I now knew how much she cared, I cared more about the constructive criticism that came my way as a piano player. To demonstrate how much she really thought of me and my ability, she informed me, as I was completing eighth grade, that it was time for me to leave her as a student. She felt she couldn't offer me what I needed to take my piano playing to another level.

If my first piano teacher were still alive, the best compliment I could give her would be to tell her one of my fondest methods of therapy as an adult is sitting down and playing piano. At times, my thirty minutes of practicing back then has stretched out to three hours nowadays when I can play. It turns out the greatest gift my parents ever gave me was piano lessons and they gave me an unexpected friend in Miss Frieda. They didn't force piano lessons down my throat. They didn't expect me to be the next Van Cliburn, they simply wanted me to have fun enjoying the wonderful gift of music, and in this case, via the piano.

Why can't the same situation consistently apply in youth sports? Why can't parents step back and let their children learn something that can follow them for a lifetime as a great way to enjoy exercise and camaraderie with friends?

Why do parents at a youth wrestling tournament have to border the mat their child is wrestling on, as if their son or daughter can't continue without the parents calling out every move? Wouldn't it be just as easy to sit in the bleachers and encourage their child? When they decide they must be on the edge of the mat, within feet of their child, it's much easier to cross the emotional line and end up being the subject of viral YouTube videos. This is what has happened on several occasions, where parents actually ended up fighting each other while the kids simply tried to participate at a youth tournament. Will these kids relish the fact their parents got in a fight at one of their youth wrestling experiences?

This is what can happen when we're afraid of allowing our kids to make mistakes, and when we feel as parents it's our job to make sure that doesn't happen. Historically, it doesn't turn out well when parents want to micromanage.

Therefore, when is the best time to allow our kids to figuratively stumble? Actually, there's nothing like the relaxing time of summer. School is out for the year, and for parents it's a time for special family trips or completion of longtime postponed projects. Perhaps putting on a new roof, resurfacing the cottage's raft, catching up on reading or maybe even putting together a book for the first time. For others, it might be time to reap the rewards from garden planting in the spring.

For athletes, summer should be a season to regenerate mind and body after a challenging school year. It should also be an opportunity to work on new aspects of a sport. It has been said that players are made in the summer. That means time needs to be put into a sport, but mistakes need to be made, too. We grow when we err.

In basketball, it may mean working on some new moves or focusing on using the opposite hand. Perhaps it's becoming a better ball-handler or leaper. Nonetheless, this time is put in on driveways or patios, in barns or in basements. It's time when kids are allowed to work on their own. Football players work on becoming stronger and more explosive, but also better passers, blockers, tacklers, or receivers. Regardless of the sport, stretching boundaries cannot be made without mistakes.

In one episode of a "60 Minutes" newscast, world-famous musician Wynton Marsalis was featured and interviewed to find out what made him a successful jazz trumpeter. Marsalis responded by saying, "If you're not making mistakes, you're not trying."

Because I wasn't the most physically gifted athlete, many of my mistakes occurred while trying to get better. Think for a minute about the way the game of baseball is set up. If you consistently fail seven out of ten times as a batter, you'll probably make it to the Hall of Fame, because a .300 hitter is considered very good. That's a lot of failure, but in baseball, it's part of what it takes to be successful.

Just like with my music, the beauty about making all my mistakes was that I was in an environment where I was encouraged to goof up and get better. I understood that making mistakes was part of the growing process.

In my travels with sports and life, I see many kids hang their heads after committing an error like it's the end of the world. It appears they feel they're a failure if they slip up.

In his videos, fitness guru and creator of the popular P90X workout, Tony Horton repeatedly said "Do your best and forget the rest." This is sage advice from someone who surely made mistakes in developing his world-renowned fitness programs.

As time passes on, competition seems to become more structured and intense. Because of that, my fear is parents and kids are losing sight of the growth opportunities in sports – all possible via mistakes. Again, these errors aren't the end of the world.

Mistakes are a blessing in our lives. When we realize their value, every day of our lives can be a bit more relaxing, no matter what season it is, or what we're attempting to do.[23]

Chapter 7

Virtues and Values

According to BibleGateway.com (http://BibleGateway.com), "Values are uncompromisable, undebatable truths that drive and direct behavior. They are motivational – they give us reasons why we do things; and they are restrictive – they place boundaries around behavior."

The saying "If you're not cheating, you're not trying" is blasphemous to good sportsmanship, yet it rings out from those who only care about winning, not necessarily how you get there. Instead, we should focus on scripture, which says, "Never tire of doing what is right."[24]

What values drive your behavior? What values would you like to drive your behavior?[25]

As kids, one of the activities we did to keep busy during the dog days of summer was play board games. Competitive juices flowed during these friendly interactions just as they did our pickup games and organized leagues. There was a phrase uttered at times at each of these venues meant to call someone out for not following the rules. "Cheaters never prosper," was the proverbial accusation of choice, and when someone did, we all knew we were being challenged for failing to do what is right.

Let's say we were playing Chutes and Ladders, a game designed with shortcuts (ladders to help you advance) and shortfalls (chutes to take you backwards) to help someone navigate the entire one hundred squares course before others. Sometimes we didn't like the number the die told us we were supposed to advance, because it was going to take us down a chute and delay our chances of winning. To improve our chances of winning, we (I) changed our (my) number of spaces to avoid the chute. This was wrong, and "cheaters never prosper" rang clear.

In pickup baseball, the challenge often surfaced when a ball headed into the corner of the neighbor's field was proclaimed to be a fair ball, much to the chagrin of the opposing team who thought it was foul. It was always difficult to tell because we didn't have painted lines on Mr. Birschbach's field.

Times like this can make sports and the games we play more stressful and tension-filled, instead of a fun-filled activity, like they're supposed to be.

Certainly, if cheating took place, it should have been brought up. Also, if we were indeed making poor decisions and not following the rules, we should be confronted. We should also be responsible enough to admit such things and realize they are wrong and make the proper adjustments. For winning a friendly neighborhood game of Chutes and Ladders, is cheating worth it? No, it's not, but somewhere along the line, I know I was one who possessed the feeling something extra had to be done in order to win. If I wasn't the winner of these games, I felt like a loser. Thankfully, I've lost that feeling of needing to cheat.

In the world of sports, my perfect birthday gift would be for the win-at-all costs mentality to finally park itself at the side of the road.

As taught by the Josephson Institute – a nonprofit organization that aims "to improve the ethical quality of society by changing personal and organizational decision making and behavior" – victory should be pursued with honor and respect.[26]

The Institute conducted a study of the relationship between high school attitudes and behavior later in life. The survey found attitudes about the need to cheat, and actual high school cheating are significant predictors of lying and cheating in many adult situations. In other words, if adults teach kids to cheat, there's a good chance the kids, too, will cheat as adults.

Nonetheless, parents of athletes are adults who are responsible for the decisions they make and should be held accountable.

When Paul Ihlenfeldt was asked to comment on the often-heard phrase regarding cheating, he reinforced what is being taught by the Josephson Institute when he proclaimed, "Cheating is too easy, and it doesn't help you. Taking shortcuts will then adversely affect you in other aspects of life." What happens when the mechanics of cheating don't work? Instead of teaching creative cheating, teach the kids the right way, the honest way, and it will teach our children how to properly address challenges that will invariably come in our lives.

The website momsteam.com offers several ideas why parents may act the way they do at youth sporting events.

These issues come from parents who:

- **Use youth sports to gratify their egos.** Some parents are bent on experiencing emotional highs, and let their emotions get the better of them, convinced that almost every kind of behavior must be tried if it helps their child or child's team be successful. When they behave like this, they feel they're identifying with their children's feelings, goals, and dreams. Unfortunately, they end up focusing on their own.

- **Are unable to cope with the emotional ups and downs of youth sports.** The roller coaster rides of competition definitely challenge our children, but they challenge us parents as well. It's clear to see, some parents cross the line of emotion and end up acting in inappropriate ways.

- **View youth sports as a competition with other parents.** We all want our kids to be successful, but some parents see parenting itself as a competition in which success depends on our child winning and others' children losing. I know I was bound and determined to have our first son walking by the time he was 10 months old because then I felt I would win as a parent.

- **See the time and money spent on their child's youth sports as an investment.** Because youth sports demand the two things that most parents have in shortest supply – money and time

– too many view these sacrifices as investments which they want to keep an eye on and protect. As one parent told me after I complimented the play of his son, "He better be for how much I spent on him."

• **Believe that lower standards of behavior apply to youth sports.** This is where it comes down to expectations. Moral reasoning seems to go out the window when we take our seats at a sporting event because that's "our place to vent," no matter how inappropriately. This is where we can make a difference. Change the expectations, change the results.

• **Have a hard time giving up control.** Many parents of athletes were athletes themselves. Therefore, there's an innate sense of competition, which is hard to let go to those involved in the event. Those who have given up that control, tend to act inappropriately to get it back.[27]

Interestingly, in my discussion with Ryan Borowicz, he countered this last point when he commented, "Most of the issues I've had with parents, come from those parents who never had their day, or their day got cut short as an athlete. The parents who I often feel have a good perspective on things, had their day. They had success. They achieved some goals and some dreams, so they don't have to live it through their kid, and I think a lot of people who got hurt in high school, or had a knucklehead coach, or just didn't quite reach the level they thought they should, now wants to do it through their kid. I see a lot of that, whereas the guys I grew up with, who are around, who had success, just sit back, just watching their kid, not super intense and let their kid talk and make decisions, because they had their day. They don't have to live through their kid. Certainly, it's anecdotal, and there certainly are exceptions, but in general, most of the guys and gals who were good athletes, and had their day, got everything out of their ability and don't have to get that out of their kids."

When we regularly practice trustworthiness, respect, responsibility, fairness, caring and citizenship – the Josephson Institute's Six Pillars of Character – we're on our way. A true sportsman is even willing to lose rather than sacrifice ethical principles to win.[28]

Therefore, let's create a set of values that will stand the test of time. Values drive our behavior and are more important to a parent's effectiveness than anything else.

Again, what values drive your behavior? What values would you like to see as your driving force? If we try to form our list by checking around us, the self-centered and politically correct moral standards of today will confuse us because the rules are continuously changing. Spending time to create our own list is worth it for parents, as well as anyone else. Whether it's also as a coach, administrator, business entrepreneur, official, etc., values are uncompromising truths that direct our behavior.

Scripture tells us we need to:

- Speak truth from our heart to help us lead an honorable life.
- Be kind and treat our neighbors with respect.
- Honor those who also seek righteousness, and keep our promises, even if they hurt.

People who use these beliefs to guide their decisions will find success. They'll be able to find a confidence that will produce emotional stability and consistency worth following. This list of core scruples can be used to tie into anyone's vision and it's important to act on these values, as compared to convenient ones. It's easy to talk about our ethics, but sometimes it can be very hard to live them out. When we uncompromisingly stick to our values, life will be very rewarding.[29]

However, even when we choose the honorable path of values and good sportsmanship, when we'll be doing nothing but living with impeccable values, we will get pushback reminding us of those confrontations of our youth. If that happens, we must be confident in the values we have developed, and we must continue forward.

During a recent conversation with one of our sons, we discussed what it looks like to be a leader at sporting events. We talked about how it can be tough at times being transparent with what you believe and trying to accomplish, knowing that you may be the recipient of rebuttals or attacks. In fact, scripture states, "Blessed are those who are persecuted because of righteousness, for theirs is the kingdom of heaven."[30] In other words, the negative pushback is a positive sign you're doing the right things in trying to fix the negative environment in sportsmanship.

The world we live in is making it harder nowadays for those who want to do what's right, because the world's definition of what is right is constantly changing, making it like shooting at a moving target. When I'm hunting, it's difficult enough for me to hit something sitting still. If the target starts moving, I'm going to have an even harder time. The best thing for parents who want to be positive leaders at sporting events is to be encouraged to continue stepping out and doing what's right. Keep confronting the negative, until the positive expectations are set. Nonetheless, for some encouragement, here is a compilation of statements called the Paradoxical Commandments.

They were created in 1968 by Kent Keith as part of a booklet for student leaders at Harvard University.

Over the course of time, Keith's commandments have traveled around the world and reportedly have been used by leaders in all walks of life. Even Mother Teresa thought the Paradoxical Commandments were important enough to put them on the wall of her children's home in Calcutta, India.

As they have for me, I hope they give all parents the courage to keep going:

- People are illogical, unreasonable, and self-centered. Love them anyway.

- If you do good, people will accuse you of selfish ulterior motives. Do good anyway.
- If you are successful, you will win false friends and true enemies. Succeed anyway.
- The good you do today will be forgotten tomorrow. Do good anyway.
- Honesty and frankness make you vulnerable. Be honest and frank anyway.
- The biggest men and women with the biggest ideas can be shot down by the smallest men and women with the smallest minds. Think big anyway.
- People favor underdogs but follow only top dogs. Fight for a few underdogs anyway.
- What you spend years building may be destroyed overnight. Build anyway.
- People really need help but may attack you if you do help them. Help people anyway.
- Give the world the best you have and you'll get kicked in the teeth. Give the world the best you have anyway.[31]

The rules at sporting events (and board games) are intended to provide for fair competition. As we've stated, sports are about having a level playing field, so everyone has the same opportunity for success. Rules set a level of expectation, and we all need to do a better job of raising the bar of good sportsmanship – of ethics. We also all need to do a better job of following through on these expectations, and that's where the Paradoxical Commandments can be helpful.

Perhaps the first preeminent golfer was Bobby Jones. When Bobby played in the early Twentieth Century, it is said he played golf for the sheer fun of the game. Reportedly, during a U.S. Open, Jones hit an errant drive into the woods. After Jones went into the woods to find his ball, he reappeared to say he was penalizing himself one stroke. Apparently, the ball had moved as he was checking to see if it was his, and the rule calls for a ball-moving penalty whether the player is being witnessed or not. This was Jones' way to honor the game of golf. Jones was surprised his act of sportsmanship received so much attention.[32] Unfortunately, someone might reason away the Jones example as old-school, and not applicable for today's society. Flash forward to the beginning of the twenty-first century to another golfer, but this time someone not nearly as famous.

Zach Nash was a teenager when he won a 2010 junior Wisconsin PGA tournament. His legendary story started after the tournament when he discovered at home, he had won the championship with one too many golf clubs in his bag. He wondered how that could be, but it turned out that prior to the tournament, a friend had dropped by, left a club at his home and Zach mindlessly threw it in his bag, probably just to get it out of the way.

When Nash realized he had violated the rules of golf, he called the Wisconsin PGA to let them know what happened. He sent back his medal, too. It was a club he didn't even use in the tournament. Nonetheless, Nash did the right thing.[33]

Historically, the game of golf has the reputation for the highest standards of sportsmanship, and unruly fans in golf are summarily escorted from the tournament – no questions asked.

If golf can pull it off, why can't all sports? Therefore, this is the sportsmanship I believe is the responsibility of all sports participants – including spectators.

What does it look like if we break the high expectations?

Remember, being competitive is fine, but being classless is not. Just because we are competitive, there is no need to turn into some sort of ugly monster. When we watch our kids compete, do we use foul language to express our support or intimidate the visiting families?

If an opponent is injured, do we do our best to show our support for the fallen, or do we express our glee that a quality opponent is out of the contest? When we win, are we gracious winners? How about when we lose?

As adults, do we seek out the parents of the opposing teams and congratulate them if their kids were better at that time? Believe me, I'm not really good at accepting defeat, and perhaps it's because

I know I still have work to do developing my own control as a parent. Nonetheless, I have self-respect, and I know I have eyes watching me. When those eyes look at the parents of our school – be it in the community or in the stands – what do they see?

I want them to see honorable parents like NBA Hall of Famer Julius Erving and his wife, who reportedly had the courage to call police and turn in their own son when they discovered he was having an underage drinking party at their home and violating the athletic code. Dr. J and his wife were gone for the evening, but still did what was right.

I want our fans to be like former NFL coach Tony Dungy, who guided his team to a Super Bowl victory without ever swearing at his players.[34] If he can do it as a coach, it surely can be accomplished as parents. Dungy would be the first to admit he isn't perfect but having the philosophy that the only avenue to player motivation is by being an intense, foul-mouthed ogre is wrong.

It would be awesome to witness the home fans welcome the opposition as they run out on the court for warm-ups. A renewed sense of spirit would also build up in that parent body to see that same set of fans say absolutely nothing, except for one "cough," while their opponents shot free throws. Then it would be even better to see that cough immediately go away because a parent stood up and made it clear it is unacceptable to slip like that.

I would enjoy seeing a section of parents and kids having so much fun focusing on cheering their own team, they wouldn't waste any of their energy trying to harass their opponents.

I know it's still going to be difficult, so let's go through a few scenarios, and see how you'd respond:

- It's crunch time and the intensity is beyond belief. Your favorite team is being challenged and the emotions are flowing. All of a sudden, the official makes a questionable call and you feel like bursting at the seams.

What do you do?

- Perhaps the game is tight, but your team is starting to make a run. The game has been a back-and-forth affair all night and your son or daughter is playing hard. You feel more confident about your team's chances of pulling out the victory, and you are tempted to turn to the opposing team's fans across the aisle and taunt them with a sarcastic clap.

What do you do?

- Maybe your team has just suffered a gut-wrenching defeat, capped by an opponent's improbable last-second play. In your administrative role, you watch the hall to monitor departing fans and you witness some of the opposing crowd leaving in an upsetting celebratory mode. You feel like grabbing some of the fans and physically confronting them.

What do you do?

- Because the pressure of a win-or-go-home environment in a single elimination tournament is greater than round-robin or double-elimination formats, the fans from your school are going absolutely crazy. You're facing a nearby rival and some of the opposing fans come up to you and question the behavior of your crowd. As a representative of your school, you feel like becoming defensive and lashing out at the accuser.

What do you do?

- As a fan at a tense contest, your team is competing at a high level with the right to go to state on the line. During a critical stretch of the game, one of your team's players makes a crucial mistake and you feel like cursing out loud.

What do you do?

Sports and life are full of stress that can lead to overwhelming emotions. We become so involved in activities that feelings can well up inside to the point they want to come out like a volcanic eruption.

Outbursts occur when we've emotionally come unglued. However, we can gain self-control over these bad habits.

According to crosswalk.com, here's how:

- Admit your struggles. Be honest with how poorly you've managed your emotions.
- Recognize that your emotions can work for you rather than against you.
- Change your thought patterns. Replace unhealthy thoughts with healthy thoughts.
- View emotionally unglued moments as wake-up calls.
- Identify your style of reacting to troubling emotions – exploding or stuffing.
- Overcome emotionally exploding. Create a response template you can use in a heated moment, so you can respond in a healthier way than spewing your emotions out.
- Overcome emotionally stuffing. Decide to deal with your emotions through honest transparency rather than stuffing them deep inside where they will change into bitterness.
- Check your motives and assumptions. Make sure they are pure.
- Make praise and thanksgiving regular habits in your life.
- Enjoy rest in your life. When you do, you'll gain the peace needed to help control your emotions.[35]

The point I'm trying to make clear for everyone is that sports should not have a separate set of rights and wrongs in the name of winning. Traditions should not necessarily be continued just because "that's the way it's always been done."

As we look to decide between existing with the old way of behavior and implementing new standards, it's important to know, the more we make the wrong choice, the harder it is to remember the right way. Also, the longer we wait to confront misdeeds, the greater it will have a hold on us.

If we wait too long, we may even forget what it means to do right. Hopefully, we're not on the verge of forgetting. Again, doing what's right will not always be the most popular decision. In fact, those who try to be honest will usually be in the minority. Also, we shouldn't be content to do what's right some of the time. We should eliminate any thoughts, practices, or possessions that prevent us from being totally committed.

Sadly, most people put their own interests first. It is also true that knowing what is right and doing what is right can be two different things. If we don't know the difference between right and wrong, we may end up doing what we think is right at the time, and that could be problematic, too. It's tough, but doing what's right should be an all-the-time habit. It needs to be a way of life – a lifestyle worth watching – and copying.[36]

Are the expectations different for parents of younger, aspiring athletes?

It shouldn't be but reaching younger parents of athletes could be perceived as more important than parents of high school aged kids. By the time they reach the upper levels of competition, you would hope they understand how to properly behave.

Unfortunately, unless someone is starting a school system from scratch, and the expectations will be established right from the first day of kindergarten, the variables in the parent formula will always be changing as families come and go. Sadly, we don't have the luxury a controlled experiment would provide.

One item easier to accept for sports at a younger age is the fact the players usually complete their celebration or sulking sooner and move on to prepare for the next time they'll be playing with their friends, whether it's the game next week or the start of next season. What's actually taking place is establishing traditions of having fun.

To support the notion of allowing our kids to lead, here's a list by Stefanie Mullen (owner and founder of Ooph.com) of ten things parents of athletes should know:

- It's not about you, it's about them. Don't live your own sports dreams through your kids. It's their turn now. Let them make their own choices, both good and bad.

- Never talk to a coach about your child's playing time after a game. Have your child do that. If you just can't help yourself, send an email the next day to ask for phone time.

- *Never* yell at referees. They're trying. How would you like it if someone came to your job and screamed at you? If you have real issues, follow through the next day.

- Do *not* coach your kid from the sideline. Be a cheerleader, not a coach. If you wanted to coach, you should have volunteered.

- It is *extremely unlikely* you are raising a professional athlete. Let them have a good time and learn the lessons they are supposed to be learning in sports.

- Kids should play the sport that is in season until they are in middle school. Then they can decide which one or two sports they want to play and become more focused. Cross training prevents injuries and burnout.

- If you have nothing nice to say, sit down and be quiet. Don't be *that* parent.

- If you are losing your mind on the sideline of a game, look in the mirror and figure out why. Put that energy into something more productive.

- Let them fail. Forgotten equipment, not working out, not practicing at home? Let them suffer the consequences of that. It will make them better.

• Your kids are watching you. Make them proud, not embarrassed.[37]

In other words, our kids want us to be there for them in a supportive, parental role, yet be a light for others and especially for them. Therefore, it's a compliment to say that someone is being a light to others.

Consider some benefits of light. First, light exposes dirt. If we live a righteous life, it will expose the shady deeds of others. Being determined to do what's right amongst those who won't, will cause culprits to feel guilty and vulnerable. Persistent integrity on our teams and in the workplace will discourage dishonesty because of strong principles.

Secondly, light illuminates our path to prevent stumbling. When we walk by righteous principles, our lives will have a greater calling and purpose, and those around us will notice. Then, the curious onlookers will be forced to make a choice – to join in and rise to new heights, or step aside and fall behind. Why do you think fewer crimes are committed during the day than at night? It's because of the light.

Light also dispels fear. Notice how plants close up at night, but eagerly open during the daytime light. Lighthouses provide a great service to ships in the dark. The nightlight in our bathrooms enables us to make our way without worrying about stubbing our toes or falling down the steps as we take care of our nighttime calling.

Those who walk in the light can be great mentors for others who may be temporarily lost. The light will be seen through kind words and good deeds. Be a determined light for others and help make our world a brighter place.[38]

Chapter 8

Humility

One character trait that helps us demonstrate the life we should live is that of humility. A humble leader doesn't flaunt his/her position of power, but instead works with the weakest member of the team to try and raise them up to a new level. A captain or leader on a team also demonstrates humility by obedience to the coach or administrator, not by trying to coach themselves or undermine what is being taught or envisioned. Lastly, a humble leader doesn't grab for power or authority, they patiently wait for the coach to increase their influence. In this world of me-first, that's a challenging stance to take, one that will probably get push-back. Nonetheless, scripture teaches us "Blessed are the meek for they shall inherit the earth."[39] Our creator admires those who are humble enough to be servant leaders, but also when we have an "others first" mentality, it's easier for us to be content with what transpires in our lives.

Do you know someone who meets the definition of a humble parent leader?

Today's world encourages people to be bold and outgoing – to serve themselves – instead of others. Therefore, humble leaders are quite often seen as passive and weak – instead of with disciplined strength and power they've gained by serving others. Humble leaders don't say "look at me." They work in anonymity while becoming the best they can be. The difficulty with humility is that as soon as you think you've got it, you've lost it.[40] Author C.S. Lewis said, "True humility is not thinking less of yourself; it is thinking of yourself less."[41]

How do accomplished leaders survive the barrage of attention after a run of success? It takes a mature person to be able to check their pride at the door with so many people cheering you on or singing your praises on a job well done. As parents, it is our job to make sure our kids stay on track, but in a humble manner. It's up to us to encourage them, but not try to live through them. We need to remember, *it's not about me.*

The aforementioned videos of parents at youth wrestling tournaments that have dotted the YouTube landscape are not flattering examples of humility, but more representative of a situation of trying to live through their kids. It's not good when you become the topic of conversation because you end up crossing the line of emotion and arguing with each other about how the other family's child is illegally wrestling, which is the official's job to determine. Can't we all humbly get along?

This reminds me when I was an alternate member of the Green Bay Packers chain crew and was able to be on the sidelines for some exciting games, it was amazing how deafening the Lambeau Field crowd noise could be after the Packers made special plays. If I was a player and knew the cheering was for me, it would have been easy to lose focus and take the credit for my team's accomplishments. However, that's not being a humble leader or a participant.

Those who try to defer the praise to teammates and spread the wealth of success understand the value of humility. It's easy to see why those who look to grab the spotlight or brag about their accomplishments, seem to "fall on their face" somewhere down the road. What they do is seek that greater influence before they're ready for it, and then they don't know how to handle it when they get it.

It should be easier to submit and be humble in times of loss or failure, but true humility comes in victory, when we're tempted to puff up our chests and gloat about how great we are. You'll be able to recognize when someone is humble or if they're still working on finding it.

I remember attending a high school basketball regional final with our oldest son at a nearby school. We went with a family friend who loves high school basketball to observe a local team who had an outstanding point guard. I had heard about his exploits and wanted to expose my son to observe what was making this young man quite the talk of high school basketball fans in our area.

The gym was packed with crazed fans from both schools, and with unbiased observers like us. Being a former point guard, I treasured watching players I felt replicated what I tried to demonstrate when I competed – a selfless combatant who looked to serve his teammates first. It didn't take me long to admire his ability to discern when he needed to serve his teammates versus looking to score himself. Running the fast break, I noticed a young man who operated under control, knowing when to take it to the basket, contrasting when to pull up and shoot the mid-range jumper. From what I could tell, he was well coached and made very few, if any, physical *or* mental mistakes in that regional final.

In fact, he was so good that night, he created enough turmoil for his opponent. That frustration boiled over, and one of the opposing team members lost his cool and was called for a technical foul. Typically, a technical is called when abusive language is used or an egregious act is committed, and the officials are working to clean up the emotions that crossed the line of poor sportsmanship. The public address announcer commenced to announce who committed the unsportsmanlike act, and that should have been the end of it. However, shortly after the name and jersey number were identified, a gentleman stood up in the stands below left of where we were sitting, and yelled out in a time of silence, "Yeah, that's *my* boy!" I was shocked by the man's response. First of all, I didn't expect any response, and then when it was clear it was the boy's father, I was embarrassed for the entire family that he would think his son had done something worth drawing attention to himself at that moment. This was not an example of heartfelt parental humility.

Sadly, for how bold the father was in standing up and demonstrating "pride" at his son's misbehavior, I'm not real confident a discussion on proper character was conducted in that family's home that night, or anytime soon thereafter.

Unfortunately, this was not an example of how a parent or adult leader should humbly support our kids and young people. Instead of the "look at me" attitude that father portrayed by standing up and drawing attention to himself, we need more individuals who have a good head on their shoulders and a servant's heart. As soon as that event took place in that contest, I turned to my son and promised him I would never embarrass him like that during a game.

How can parents train their children to have the proper humble, self-giving attitude in sports and in life? It all starts at home, and here are a few tips from Jill Rigby's book "Raising Unselfish Children in a Self-Absorbed World:"

- **Take a hard look at ourselves.** As parents, we should be the most important role model in the lives of our children. Are we setting a humble example worth following? Is our lifestyle selfish or selfless? Do we rationalize our mistakes? Do we make excuses or blame others? We need to serve without expecting something in return, display courage – not bitterness – and love our children unconditionally. Empower them by explaining it's okay to make mistakes – just stay humble and teachable.

- **Look out the window, not in the mirror**. If we help our kids look beyond themselves to be humble and help others, we will take away self-centeredness and encourage self-respect. This healthy disposition leads to well-functioning adults instead of those with feelings of fragile entitlement.

- **Build family togetherness**. By strengthening relationships at home, a child's sense of security grows and encourages them to reach out to others. The family meal is an incredible bonding tool. Put sports in their place instead of chasing kids to tournaments every weekend. Go on a family camping trip or take time to catch a matinee – complete with popcorn and soda. What about bowling using the bumpers – even for mom and dad and big kids? Quality time can't be planned – it comes during quantity time.

- **Provide opportunities to give back.** Teach kids to count their blessings by writing thank-you notes or shaking someone's hand. Find time to deliver homeless shelter want-list items or volunteer to help shut-ins, perhaps just by shooting the breeze. By encouraging our kids to tutor a younger student needing a little help and a friend, you teach them how to be humble and show compassion and empathy towards others.[42]

Even when it appears we are on the right path in life, feeling pretty good about ourselves, and seem to have everything in order at home, something invariably comes along and provides a reality check.

For instance, when I was a sixth-grade football player, I hadn't really sprouted yet athletically or physically, so any accomplishments I was fortunate to encounter were more from the result of giving it my best than anything else. I had the opportunity to benefit from some special coaches who put in quite a bit of their time and were intent on helping us experience memories for a lifetime. At one practice, one of our assistants told us, "Be sure to give it your all every day on every play, so when you look back as an adult, you won't have to wish you tried harder as a kid." Being pretty small and skinny at the time, I bought into that battle cry right from the beginning and gave it my all at every practice and in every game.

Therefore, when the opportunity presented itself to score a wide-open touchdown by racing down the far sideline during one of our games, I felt like it was all coming together. My hard work was paying off. *Every day on every play* put into action. Nonetheless, my success temporarily came to a screeching halt, when a faster seventh grader tackled me from behind. Not only was he able to catch me, but he also jumped on my back and tackled me directly on top of the ball. I subsequently squirmed on the grass gasping for the air that was squeezed out of my thin body, embarrassed for not being able to cash in on my opportunity. I had been humbled by another's superior ability, but then humility hit me again when my father approached from the sideline, scooped me up in his arms, and carried me to the bench area. *Oh man!* I was thinking, *if I'm going to be this big, tough football player, I should be walking to the sideline myself.*

Doses of humility are good for us, even if we don't feel that way in the moment. True humility comes when people recognize their gifts and strengths and are willing to use them to help others. My dad had a servant's mentality, and as I look back, I don't blame him for wanting to help me. Remember, he had a father who didn't outwardly show a lot of love and wanted to improve on that in his family. My dad didn't care one iota about the fact I was in that point of my life where I was trying to be a little more macho than the day before. He just cared about helping his son. Pride is concerned about who is right, whereas humility is more concerned about what is right. I believe Dad got it right because of his humility. One thing for sure, the next time I got the wind knocked out of me, I didn't spend nearly as much time writhing in agony before peeling myself up off the field and walking off under my own power.

Sometimes we're humiliated because success goes to our head, or we temporarily lose our mind and say stupid things.

Ideally, all our lessons would come from our parents, but when that doesn't happen, teachers can provide helpful lessons of humility when they're needed, and they can be lessons we use throughout our own lives that include sporting experiences for our kids or grandkids. In fifth grade, my favorite elementary teacher brought me down a few pegs after an afternoon recess filled with pick-up basketball, where I felt my success was worthy of everyone knowing. Not only was she not impressed with what she was hearing, she also made me fully aware of her feelings that pick-up basketball was nothing worth gloating over and not something to give me reason to cause bad feelings in others. Certainly, I didn't enjoy the chastisement I received, but I deserved it. What I needed to do in the first place was fight the temptation to allow popularity or success to twist my perception of my own importance. It's much easier to be humble when we're not on center stage, but how do we react to high praise and rewards, especially when we become older and it involves our children?

You'd think a lesson like that would stick with me, however, it didn't have as long a lasting effect as my teacher probably desired, because in seventh grade a classmate of mine and I visited the bathroom during a break in classroom activity. In the hall, we came across one of the school custodians, and we said hi to him and called him by his first name. Nowadays, I know there are schools who allow this to happen, but our school system taught us to address any teacher or school employee as Mr., Miss, or Mrs. That day, we did not address that particular custodian with the proper respect our school was expecting, and we should have been offering.

In the bathroom, we began to conduct our business, when our middle school reading teacher walked into the bathroom. He had heard our disrespectful address to our school custodian, and he was there to correct it. At that point in my life, he was a very tall man with hands that seemed to be as big as baseball gloves; he commanded respect simply with his presence.

He began by trying to clarify what he heard us say and how we said it. He asked us if we had indeed called the custodian by his first name. I immediately denied it, but my classmate rightfully came clean and admitted his disrespect. Why did I lie?

Nonetheless, my dose of humble pie delivered that day may have been as big as any I've endured in my life, and I deserved every bit of it. Not only was I disrespectful to the custodian, but then I lied about it. How bad is that? Thankfully, our school's reading teacher confronted me, provided a valuable lesson in character development, and produced the humility I needed to get better as a young man. Obviously, I've never forgotten the lesson I learned that day. It's interesting to note his role in the school district eventually shifted to the high school while I was there, and I was able to bring that experience up to him and thank him for confronting me the way he did. We ended up having a good laugh about it because I had learned from it.

These two teachers demonstrated what is possible when following through with students. It also tells me what can happen when we confront older "students," that is, parents.

At times, it seems humility has become extinct like the dodo bird, especially in sports. There is greater push by parents for their kids to excel in sports, and with the price of college rising dramatically, it may be to pursue the almighty athletic scholarship.

We must remember it's not being passive or a sign of weakness to be humble, and through no coincidence, there is a renewed commitment by most college coaches to recruit kids with top-notch character. I've even heard where college coaches will *not* recruit certain kids if the parents seem like they could pose challenges the coaches would rather avoid. Robert Brooks mentioned how even at the highest levels of sports, like the NFL, greater focus is being placed on improving character in the league, thus increasing the value of those, like chaplains, whose role is to help individuals improve their approach to everyday life.

A humble leader doesn't flaunt his or her position or status. A humble leader also doesn't impose his or her will on others but submits to the good of the whole. Thirdly, a humble leader doesn't grab for power or position. He or she patiently waits for their influence to increase. Lastly, a truly humble person has a disciplined strength and a selfless aura that should be admired by all.

As an ancient proverb states, "It's not good to eat too much honey, and it's not good to seek honors for yourself."[43] If we live a life of moderation while continually striving to be the best we can be, the accolades will take care of themselves. In other words, if we get it right on the inside, everything will be fine on the outside.[44]

There is a variety of ways to experience humility, and it's amazing how different a person's humility formula can differ from the next. We can touch on a handful of ways of experiencing humility by simply looking at our lives and thinking of ways to be humbled. I've already addressed some, but times of illness and injury can make us take a second look at how we approach life and knock us down a few pegs.

One summer, shortly after I moved on from college, I was participating in a summer basketball league and decided I was going to take a charge on a hard-driving opponent. I established my defensive position a bit early, and it was noticed by the confident young man who put his head down and rammed me with his shoulder and a little extra energy. It caused me to awkwardly fall backwards, preventing me from properly sliding on my shorts, but allowed me just enough time for a last-ditch effort of putting my hands back to brace myself. Unfortunately, the force of the collision with the floor caused one wrist to be sorer than the other. It turned out, one wrist was broken, and the other sprained. As a lefty, I always prided myself in being able to go both ways in attacking the basket, but after this incident, I was relegated to be a one-handed ballplayer, and for 6-8 weeks, it turned out to be my opposite hand. The accident took place in the first half, and at halftime, I realized with my first left-handed attempt I was relegated to being a righty for a while. When you temporarily lose your writing hand, your main shooting hand, or even your tooth brushing hand, you realize how lucky you are when two hands work together wonderfully. The humility experienced through this injury helped me better appreciate each future healthy moment and show empathy for others when they get hurt.

Humility can also be taught through other mistakes, which athletes often encounter by watching game films. When this happens, we need to approach these sessions with a proper perspective, knowing we can get better if we improve by learning from our mistakes. If we don't humbly approach these sessions, it's going to be tough to even realize mistakes were made. No one likes to be exposed, but through a little lost face, so to speak, we can get better before the next contest, or even the next season. When our favorite team's season ends prematurely, and doesn't reach the championship game, the offseason begins, and re-evaluation of the season, of techniques, drills, play-calling if it applies, etc. Coaches may attend clinics to learn new methods of reaching players, and players could go to camps to find ways to get better. Talks at home with family members or on vacations, or on retreats help people recharge the batteries of life.

Years ago, when writing my sportsmanship column, the news service would include my email address for anyone with questions or comments. Sure enough, I received both, and the confrontations weren't nearly as fun as the compliments. Nonetheless, when looked at in the right way, the humility these contributions of criticism provide can be used as an opportunity to self-reflect and as motivation to get better and to persevere. When we get pushback, we have to decide *how* we're going to react to our challenges, which help us prioritize what's most important.

Let's look at five ways we can experience humility.

- **Illness or Injury.** Sickness and injury really shake us up. They help re-evaluate our fragility, because life's view from bed or from behind a plaster cast is quite different. Appreciate each moment and show empathy for others.

- **Mistakes**. We often think pretty highly of ourselves. When we think we did well in a game, watching game film might change our tune. Our goal should be to have the right perspective of our performances. A team reviewing film provides a collective examination of efforts. No one likes to be exposed, but humility enables correction before the next contest. Even though a little face might be lost, everyone is far better off from the humble lessons of the present.

- **Design**. Sometimes, humility needs to be implemented by design to offer reflection. For coaches or players it can be the off-season. This is meant to be a time of recharging the battery or gaining new information to become better. Vacations, retreats, camps, or clinics are all designed with this in mind. We live in an age of distractions and finding a time to get better at what we do, or simply get away, are important. Keeping a journal to learn from humbling experiences can be beneficial.

- **Attacks**. Personal attacks can humble our lives. If we look at criticism the right way, we can benefit greatly. Experiences strengthen our confidence when we use them as motivation to get better and to persevere.

- **Death.** People often don't like to talk about death. Nonetheless, Pearl Harbor and 9/11 might have been two of the most humbling experiences of our time. Our security was penetrated in two different ways, and we felt control was lost. All our achievements will one day be over and old age reminds us through aching bones, sore shoulders, and glasses. Each reminder helps us get a better view of life and death. Wise people see that glory and fame are meaningless over the course of time and our achievements will be blips that no one will notice or remember. Death can shake us up so we put our worldly pursuits in proper order.[45]

Poet Alexander Pope stated, "A man should never be ashamed to own that he has been in the wrong, which is but saying in other words that he is wiser today than he was yesterday."[46]

A great example of a humble leader happens to be a young man, who if not for COVID-19, would probably have entered our homes during the 2020 Tokyo Olympics. If our youth can set examples of humility for us adults, so be it. It seems more often than not, the kids get it before the adults do, *or* somewhere along the line, adults lose it. This young man isn't your typical kid – you could say he's a sports prodigy. Being a sports prodigy comes with a unique set of issues. Not only does stardom come at an earlier age, it's accompanied by the expectations to be even better than might be possible. I would say Tiger Woods was a golf prodigy, who was expected to shatter all of golf's career records. When coming out of college, Tiger took the golfing world by storm, and set workout standards golfers of the past never encountered. However, because of some personal and physical issues of his own, he hasn't been able to accomplish it quite yet, and now his recent automobile accident could dampen those chances even more.

Being a sports prodigy isn't something that can be created, bought, or hyped by parents, relatives or even the athletes themselves, because the talent level of a prodigy is clearly much higher than other athletes in that sport.

When 15-year-old Michael Phelps arrived on the international swimming scene at the 2000 Sydney Olympics, he was the talk of the town, because of his age and his ability. It seems he has passed the swimming prodigy baton to another young man, who was also 15 years old, when he surfaced nationally from outside Philadelphia.

Not only was Reece Whitley young to be a great swimmer, but he was 6'8" and towered over Phelps by 4 inches when he burst onto the scene. Whitley began swimming around age 7, could dunk a basketball and was an almost unhittable pitcher by age 13, but now holds numerous national age-group records in the pool. All the while his success continues to mount, Whitley's love and advocacy of swimming remains consistently the same. When Whitley met Michael Phelps for the first time, the two discussed staying humble and never being too satisfied with goals.

In other words, stay humble, stay hungry.

Although Whitley certainly practices hard and continues to set goals, he's quick to point out what he feels is most important when he said, "Making an impact on a young swimmer at a meet is probably more important than the times that you swim. All these records are meant to be broken, but if you change a kid's life or if you put a smile on a kid's face because you took a picture with them, that never dies."

That is pretty special advice, no matter what your age. However, that came out of the mouth of a 15-year-old Reese Whitley. Whitley's talent, humility, and willingness to mentor younger athletes in his sport are the reasons why Sports Illustrated chose him to be the recipient of their 2015 SportsKid of the Year award.

It appears Whitley is behaving how the ideal sports prodigy should handle themselves – not by bragging and spouting off, but with dignity, humility and class.[47] Many parents can learn a thing or two from young people like Reese Whitley.

In addition, if we can admit our mistakes, or that we have room for improvement in anything we're trying to accomplish, we've already humbly submitted ourselves and are moving in the right direction. Does humility immediately fix all ills? No, but it's the start needed to get going again. Accomplishments are wonderful things when thought of properly, so, again, stay humble, and stay hungry, purposely controlling our ego and continuing to strive toward success, especially when we're supporting our younger ones we love.

Chapter 9

Encouragement

The tongue is often described as the strongest muscle in our body. Actually, it consists of *sixteen* muscles. Because much of the surface is covered in taste buds, it is the primary organ of taste. With its wide variety of possible movements, the tongue also assists in forming the sounds of speech. When used properly, the tongue helps us do things like eating and vocalization, but hopefully, not at the same time. It is used to lick ice cream, blow bubbles, and whistle. Injuries *to* the tongue are very painful. Pain caused *from* the tongue is even worse.

An ancient proverb states the tongue has the power of life and death.[48] In other words, what we say has the power to motivate or destroy, energize or deflate, inspire or create despair. This is especially true with kids in sports. Young athletes are looking to please their parents and coaches, and positive affirmations will set them forward on the right path. Failure to affirm will produce over-achievement to prove worth, or underachievement to prove the accuracy of what may have been said years ago, or as recent as yesterday. I know a successful businessman, who was told as a child he wouldn't amount to anything and is spending the balance of his emotional bank account trying to prove his naysayer(s) wrong. There's nothing wrong with using people's words to motivate us to greater things, but when it causes emotional angst, then we need to take a step back and perhaps get some help.

The end of February and March provide some of the most exciting moments in sports when the "Big Dance" takes place. As we mentioned earlier, when the NCAA Men's Basketball Tournament was cancelled in 2020, we knew as a country we were experiencing a time of challenge. Normally, this is a crazy time where people plop in front of the TV and watch a lot of basketball. This joy is what all sports should provide on a consistent basis because they are games or contests. They should be outlets for exercise, teamwork, fellowship – a hopeful and safe environment of fun. Yet, our society appears to be more and more under pressure from life's issues, and it seems our kids are bearing much of that burden.

My brother-in-law used to coach eighth-grade girls' basketball when his daughter was on the team. At that time, he lost a girl from his team to suicide. I was told it was one of three Milwaukee-area suicides on the same day. Regardless of where they take place, the hurt is felt by many. Only a couple of weeks earlier, the father of the girl pleaded for any ideas to help with his depressed daughter. Her only other sibling – her older sister – committed suicide the year before. Can you imagine the pain she must have been experiencing? Can you empathize with the relatives left behind – especially the father?

Why does it seem our kids have little hope? The fun of sports should be a great release for such pain. This eighth-grade girl's father encouraged her to be in basketball to deal with her sister's death. Apparently, it wasn't enough.

Hopelessness knows no stereotypical child. These kids come from broken families, as well as solid, functional families. They are kids failing miserably in school, as well as those who are flourishing. Somehow, they are experiencing incredible pressure and don't know how to work their way through it.

As responsible adults, we need to make sure we aren't putting undue pressure on our kids, so they feel there's only one way out. We need to make sure this doesn't happen in sports. Are we putting our kids in lose-lose situations by expecting them to win every game? Is their success judged by whether their name and/or picture get in the paper? Do we love them just as much when they win as when they lose? Again, we need to look at ourselves in the mirror.

I must admit, there have been times, and still are, when I'm not fond of myself on the way home after my kids' games. When this happens, I feel like I lost control a couple of times and blurted out some things I shouldn't have said. It may not have been directed at the other team or an official, but that doesn't matter.

Sometimes, I make the mistake of being too much of a coach with my boys. When they lose a hard-fought game, they need someone to lean on. When they win a hard-fought game, they're looking for appreciation and encouragement.

What are you providing your kids? I pray its spelled h-o-p-e.[49]

During the summer between my high school sophomore and junior years, I was looking for hope from a different source, as our varsity basketball coach predicted who was going to be in the following year's starting lineup, and announced captains, too. When my name wasn't included with either the prediction or the proclamation, I admittedly was miffed. How could he forecast what was going to happen that summer? How did he know who would improve the most? At the time of his announcement, he didn't know I was going to grow four inches, and because of the motivation created by his empty prediction, I used his words and actions as motivation to become a completely different player than the year before, and much better than the one who was expected to be a captain.

In that situation, what I viewed as carelessness by this revered teacher and coach encouraged me to take a huge step forward. I used his lack of long-term thinking to my benefit, instead of letting it get me down. Unfortunately, he has passed away, and I'll never be able to check with him to verify if perhaps his words were carefully and brilliantly conducted to positively impact his program. It's possible, right?

Speaking of coaches, let's compare two well-known coaches and their methods of motivation. When Bob Knight retired, he had won more NCAA Division I men's basketball games than any other coach. However, with his history of temper tantrums directed at officials and players, you can be sure he didn't always use the most desirable language to express his opinions.

Tony Dungy and the Indianapolis Colts won Super Bowl XLI and we already mentioned how it is well-documented Dungy's

approach consisted of praise and encouragement while never raising his voice or using profanity. Is there a best way?

Renowned psychologist Erik Erikson believed every human
being goes through eight stages of life to reach his or her full
development. Stages 4 and 5 are the stages that cover the years
our kids participate in youth sports. Stage 4 is the range during
which children seek the virtue of competence by doing. From
about ages 6-11, parents and coaches need to teach young athletes
how to work through difficult situations and make decisions –
helping kids understand behaviors have consequences attached
to them.

Children need to learn from, rather than feel defeated by, mistakes. This is a time in a child's life when they need to feel special, so tell them they are valuable even when they make mistakes,
because mistakes are opportunities to learn. Encourage independent thinking – to be strong – but remind them help is available.
Stage 5 ranges on up to about 18 years of age and is the time when
the virtue of fidelity is sought. These adolescent years are when
our young athletes are concerned about their identity – how they
appear to others. It is a time when kids focus on being accepted.

These young athletes need to know they should love who they
are, because they are one of a kind. Parents and coaches need to
help them become the person and athlete they are capable of being.
Additionally, we need to encourage them to be faithful to com-
mitments – to be honest and dependable. Work with children and
players to be persistent, so dreams and goals can be reached.

Many well-intentioned parents and coaches strive to provide
these environments, but technically fail and cause emotional
damage.[50] If we give our tongue a self-examination, we should be
asking these questions. Do our words give life? Do they inspire
and challenge others to greatness? Today's goal should be to lift
someone up today with our tongue.

Here's a great example of parental support from biblegateway.
com: The five-year-old soccer goalie of Team One was an outstanding athlete, but he was no match for three or four on Team Two

who were also very good, and they began to score on him. The goalie gave it everything he had, recklessly throwing his body in front of incoming balls, trying valiantly to stop them.

After the third goal was scored against him, he could see it was no use; he couldn't stop them. He didn't quit, but he became quietly desperate. Futility was written all over him.

After the fourth goal, the little boy needed help so badly, and there was no help to be had. He retrieved the ball from the net and handed it to the referee. Then he fell to his knees and cried the tears of the helpless and broken-hearted.

His father ran onto the field and said, "Scotty, I'm so proud of you. You were great out there. I want everybody to know that you are my son."

"Daddy," the boy sobbed, "I couldn't stop them. I tried, Daddy, I tried and tried, and they scored on me."

"Scotty, it doesn't matter how many times they scored on you. You're my son, and I'm proud of you. I want you to go back out there and finish the game. I know you want to quit, but you can't. And, son, you're going to get scored on again, but it doesn't matter. Go on, now." The little guy ran back onto the field, and they scored two more times, but it was okay. This is the perfect example of an encouraging parent.[51]

Whenever Ryan Borowicz conducts a teaching session of fundamentals at his basketball school, he likes to give the kids words of encouragement, specifically including a story to help the kids relate to the intended lesson. Collegiately trained to be a teacher, Borowicz, a father of three boys himself, knows when he has a kid's attention and when he doesn't. He also understands kids aren't going to remember everything, but he loves it when kids come back years later and are able to remember a helpful anecdote that was used as a teaching tool in one of the sessions at The Driveway.

What does it look like when a coach crosses the emotional line and sends the wrong message to his team?

Years ago, I received a report that a coach called timeout during a high school football game and verbally blasted his players without regard for language. Reportedly, the officials didn't penalize him, even though there was supposed to be zero tolerance for swearing.

In a game when I was helping a friend's crew as a substitute football official, I penalized the head coach for profanely confronting his players. I threw my flag, pointed right at him, and announced the violation to our crew chief. A couple of minutes later, the coach announced to his team he had made a mistake. I could tell he was sorry.

There is absolutely no need to use this type of language to "motivate" players. Robert Brooks forwarded a related story about a former professional football coach who, during a telecast in his active days, was witnessed by his mother of using foul language. A few days later, this coach received a letter in the mail from his mother, chastising him for using improper language. It greatly affected him, and he sought advice to permanently change his verbal ways while coaching. Is it obvious how positive reinforcement from people important to us can make a huge difference in our values and our lives?

Here is a story to demonstrate how kind words can last a lifetime.

A teacher assigned her students to list the names of the others in the room on two sheets of paper, leaving a space between each name. They were to write down the nicest thing about each of their classmates. It took the entire class period to finish their assignment. Over the weekend, the teacher listed each student on a separate sheet of paper and itemized all of the compliments for each individual. The lists were distributed during the next class. Soon, the entire class was smiling.

"Really?" one whispered. "I never knew I meant anything to anyone!" "I didn't know others liked me so much."

The papers were never mentioned again in class. However, might the students have discussed the assignment with friends or parents? Regardless, the exercise had accomplished its mission. The students were happy with themselves and one another.

Several years later, one of the students was killed in Vietnam and his teacher attended the funeral. The church was packed with friends and family. After the funeral, most of the former classmates went to the luncheon. The young man's mother and father were there, waiting to speak with his teacher.

"We want to show you something," his father said, as he took out a wallet. "They found this when he was killed. We thought you might recognize it." He carefully removed two worn pieces of notebook paper that had been taped, folded, and refolded many times. The teacher knew without looking the papers were the ones on which she had listed all the good things the classmates had said about him.

"Thank you so much for doing that," the mother said. "As you can see, he treasured it."

All the classmates started to gather around. One smiled sheepishly and said, "I still have mine. It's in the top drawer of my desk at home." One student's wife said, "We have his in our wedding album." "I have mine too," one of the girls said. "It's in my diary." Then another classmate reached into her purse and showed her worn and frazzled list to the group. "I carry this with me at all times – I think we all saved them."

The teacher sat down and cried.

As parents, these stories of coaches and teachers are great reminders we need to tell the people we love and care for, that they are special and important, and we should do it before it's too late.[52]

Honestly, we should also be reaching out to our fellow citizens as a beacon of light when we're at school, the supermarket, or out on the walking trail. However, have you noticed it's become more challenging to reach out to someone and say 'Hi?' How often do you try at the grocery store, and you don't even get a grunt in return? How many times have you held the door for someone, and you get nary an acknowledgement? Have you noticed how much easier it is to unscrupulously and irresponsibly complain through our electronics? Scott Venci surmised, "Social media has given a platform to irresponsible, immature people that have uninformed opinions, which will make improving the sportsmanship environment even more difficult." As a result of technology like this, we seem to be more isolated in our lives, making it more difficult to encourage our fellow man.

Does it mean we stop trying? Absolutely not. What is the simplest form of encouragement that has existed in life and in sports for a long time? The handshake.

There are many theories as to when the handshake began, or what it was originally intended for. Nonetheless, it has evolved to be a gesture of encouragement in the form of the hand slap, high five, butt slap, and bumps that include your fist, elbow, and even your entire body. Few functions we perform are more important than keeping hope alive. Nothing can lift someone up faster than acknowledgement and encouragement for a good try. It indicates someone's effort was noticed and appreciated.

When I was a Marquette University basketball walk-on, I relished the daily scrimmages we'd have to finish our practices. As a walk-on who didn't get in very often, these were my games, and I got to play against some of the best competition in the country. Our assistant coaches, Rick Majerus and Ric Cobb, would lead the two evenly divided teams, while Coach Hank Raymonds would stroll around the court, observing from a distance. When we're off at college, coaches quite often take up the role our parents normally provide.

With that in mind, Coach Majerus was one of the best storytellers I've ever known and a blast to go out with for pizza, but when you stepped on the court, he was all business and reserved with his praise. Therefore, when I walked off the court after a scrimmage and he extended his hand to me in a congratulatory manner, I knew without a doubt I had done a good job that day. The power of encouragement, of a compliment, especially through a handshake, is amazing. Here are four tips from cbn.com on how to give a valuable compliment:

- **Be specific.** Memorable compliments are specific. Notice what it is that compelled you to want to give the compliment in the first place, and then articulate it to the person.

- **Acknowledge their character.** When complimenting an accomplishment, don't just acknowledge what the person did. Acknowledge who they had to be to accomplish it. In other words, what did it take for them to make it happen? Point to a person's character traits, such as perseverance, kindness, thoughtfulness, loyalty, humor, calmness, creativity, or courage.

- **Be authentic.** If you don't really mean the compliment, don't give it. Everyone has some character strength or gift worth of acknowledgement. Make a habit of finding the good in others. Sometimes you may be the only person to point it out.

- **Express your appreciation.** When complimenting someone about something they did that benefited you, be direct in your praise. You might assume that the people in your life know you appreciate them, but don't leave them wondering. Say so.[53]

For parents, this specific, authentically expressed encouragement comes through hugs, pats on the back, and verbal compliments. It also comes through being a great listener, which may not include any words at all, but is a wonderful form of encouragement because we're indicating our children are important enough to give them our undivided attention for that moment in time. Life can be quite challenging, even without sports. However, for us to keep fighting the good fight, we all need encouragement.

Quite often, it appears our kids know exactly how to encourage each other. For instance, at the next sporting event you attend, or watch on TV, see if the substitute player coming in slaps hands with the replaced player. Some may think it's only symbolic, but it's unifying and uplifting to the player going out. If words aren't exchanged, it's like saying, "Hey, good job. Take a well-deserved rest. I've got it from here for a while."

When we see someone in the store or on the street, instead of scowling or being all about staying to ourselves, try smiling and offering a greeting to the next person you meet – maybe even extending an encouraging hand. I'd wait with the high five, butt slap or body bump until you know a person better, but it doesn't mean we can't reach out to someone and try to lift them up for that moment and that day. It should make them feel good, and it'll definitely make you feel good, if you can get past the fear of humility involved with a possible rejection.[54]

If you really want to humble yourself, take a walk, with or without your dog, near a busy road during your community's version of rush-hour traffic. Will anyone notice you? Will anyone beep? Would anyone stop if something happened to you? If we look at ourselves as an unimportant cog in the giant wheel of society, we'll be humbled indeed.

However, we need to take stock of how unique we are and what we have to offer this world. We also need to realize how much of a difference we can, and do, make in people's lives. Just when we think we're only one in a million in this vast world, we need to remember there's a great chance we mean a million to one, and it starts at home.

As we all know, a puzzle isn't complete when one piece is missing, an engine isn't running at full-efficiency when a part is lost, and the world will keep going when we are gone – but it won't be the same. That's why we need to make the most of our opportunities to help others – especially our kids and family members – because you never know how long they're going to be around. When my wife's grandmother passed away, we reminisced about the positive things she would offer every time we saw her.

Because of where she lived, we typically only saw her around Christmastime. However, it became a tradition we cherished, because we knew she would impart some wisdom along with her witty sense of humor. It's comforting visiting someone you know will consistently lift you up.

At one time, one of my older boys forwarded me a link to an HBO documentary movie called "State of Play: Trophy Kids." The movie followed four different sports family stories where the parents were trying to live vicariously through their children with different degrees of pressure being forced on the kids. Without hesitation, you would say these were pushy parents. In fact, they caused so much stress on their kids, it became uncomfortable for me to watch. Whether it was the basketball father belittling his son and cursing the referees, or the golf father bouncing from one emotion to the next, swearing one minute at his little daughter under his breath and the next minute admitting he couldn't praise his daughter for fear of her becoming soft. From the tennis mother who practically shamed her sons into wanting to become the Number 1 doubles team in the world, to the football father who berated his son to the point of tears. These were real-life scenarios where I felt terribly for the kids.

Robert Brooks offered comments on these types of situations when he said, "Parents try to manufacture passion in their kids, which you really can't do. It needs to come from the individual who wants to get better and see how far their best can take them. Parents can get overbearing when they overstep their bounds with expectations, like our kids owe us something, especially if they make it to the pros." Brooks went on to say, "It's sad, because it's taking the fun out of the games, and the camaraderie, because kids get selfish based on parents' expectations."

Had I acted irresponsibly with my older boys, or was I causing similar stress to my youngest two? With parents acting like they did in the HBO movie, you can see why some kids don't want to pursue sports for very long.[55] However, the value of sports in kids' lives is proven by the following statistics from UP2US, an organization dedicated to help improve the lives of America's youth through sports.

- Student-athletes are four times more likely to attend college.
- Students who play sports are on time to school more and absent less.
- Student-athletes prove to be better at managing emotions, resolving conflicts, and resisting peer pressure.

- Female athletes are three times more likely to graduate than non-athletes.

Additional stats demonstrating the value of sports comes from the Women's Sports Foundation, where it stated female high school athletes are 92 percent less likely to get involved with drugs, 80 percent less likely to get pregnant and 3 times more likely to graduate than non-athletes.

A Northeastern University study showed over 70 percent of athletes aged 5-18 will drop out of sports by age 13, because they're not having fun anymore. The American College of Sports Medicine reported students who took part in more vigorous sports like soccer or football performed nearly 10 percent better in math, science, English, and social studies classes.

When parents properly support and coaches teach sportsmanship and the proper fundamentals of a particular sport, they encourage the athletes to succeed. The confidence athletes develop as they work through challenges and experience successes will be experiences they take with them into the adult working world.[56]

Remember, our time is short, and we may only have an opportunity to be a million to one. If we miss out on our opportunity, are we just one in a million? People have the opportunity to make an encouraging impact every day.

In fact, those who are giving their best in their callings in life are not only encouraging to others but are people making history. Parents, teachers, students, coaches, doctors, police officers, and firefighters all have the power to affect history by positively carrying out their lives. Whether it's at work or in sports, we can affect the paths of history with our signs of affection. People who do this won't be famous to the masses, but they'll be famous in their own little corner of the earth. They might even be famous to only one person. It makes no difference, because these are the encouraging history makers who matter.[57]

Therefore, think of those around you, including those who crossed your path in the past, and who comes to mind if you were asked to identify someone you identify as an encourager? Who epitomized the ultimate positive attitude, no matter what situation presented itself? Was it a parent? Maybe a coach or teacher jumps into your memory as the ideal encourager.

From professional sports, one of the first encouraging faces I pictured was that of former Los Angeles Dodgers manager Tommy Lasorda – who at one time was arguably baseball's most popular ambassador. I remember one Major League Game of the Week when Lasorda was still coaching third base before succeeding long-time Dodgers manager Walter Alston. Lasorda wore a microphone during the game, and he was a nonstop character of chatter. Of course, he had incentive to be talkative, knowing he was going to be featured on television. However, I think most baseball enthusiasts will agree that Tommy Lasorda came across as a genuine slap-on-the-back kind of person.

Few functions a leader will perform are as important as the one that is intended to keep hope alive.

I think a well-written third-base coach job description would include that the ideal candidate needs to be a die-hard encourager. Aside from passing signs to the hitter and baserunners, they try to do whatever they can to encourage the offense into a scoring frenzy. If there was a job description for parents, being a die-hard encourager would also be on their list, in good times *and* bad.

A die-hard encourager knows how to react when others are down and out, or frustrated and desperate, driving away darkness and doubt with a positive approach for what lies ahead. The encourager fills those around them with optimism regarding themselves, others, and the future of all those concerned. Uncannily, they know when to come alongside someone and give a boost. They are even able to discern if someone needs a quick admonition or a shoulder to borrow.

Lasorda seemed to sustain hope by offering words of encouragement. He appeared to be very good at it by using it to lead the Dodgers to eight division titles and two World Series championships when he was their manager from 1976 to 1996. People pay lots of money to hear motivational speakers, but are those people genuine encouragers?

Former baseball colleague Danny Ozark once said, "Tommy was a great motivator. He treated his players and coaches tremendously, and everyone on the team would do anything for him."

True leaders are consistent in their demeanor by offering daily encouragement.

When the world throws us difficulties, we sometimes are figuratively knocked down – gasping for breath. Surrounding ourselves with encouragers helps us remain faithful, focused, and determined to finish the race of life. Encouragement in sports is like the blowing wind for a sailboat – it keeps us moving forward. We all need that.

Lasorda was once quoted, "The difference between the impossible and the possible lies in a person's determination." He also said, "There are three types of baseball players: Those who make it happen, those who watch it happen and those who wonder what happened." This can be applied to all walks of life.

When surrounded by encouragers, the impossible seems much more possible, and we proceed as more hopeful. What type of person will you be to make a difference in this world – a discourager or an encourager?[58]

Chapter 10

Sports Should Be Fun

Being from a climate where it's a big deal when the mercury inches upward and the days get longer, the number of people spending time outside increases, and so do the practices for summer sports. With that comes a little reminder. Children and sports make a great combination – when put together properly. The physical benefits alone can pave the way for a healthy, active adulthood. Because doing our best in sports can build tremendous confidence and self-esteem, the mental development of a child also can benefit. Add to that the life lessons of responsibility, teamwork, commitment and hard work and we have a pretty good formula for what sports can do for our kids.

Somewhere along the line, our society has taken the perfect formula and distorted it from an "it's not whether you win or lose, but how you play the game" algorithm to a "win at any cost" maxim. What started out as a great way to learn the benefits of winning and losing has turned into a stressful environment that's chasing kids away. This pressure-packed atmosphere used to exist only in professional sports. Now it resides in every level of competition, including the youth sports training grounds. The athletic fields are places where kids want to have fun, but adults sometimes have ulterior motives. Parents filling the bleachers and the sidelines to cheer on their kids would be simply awesome, if it stopped right there. Then the most important adults in our kids' lives would be acting like they're supposed to – as parents.

It is unfortunate, but their exuberance usually spills over into yelling at coaches, officials and even their own kids. Multiply that by the fact that the coaches do their share of yelling at everyone, and we have a whole lot of screaming going on. Who wants to be part of that atmosphere? Summer is the perfect time for development.

It's obvious why more and more kids get burnt out at an early age. It would be so much easier if realistic goals were established and pursued by all parties involved. Is a summer league worth building walls amongst family and/or community members? Pursuing wins is fine, but if a child has given his/her best, it's okay to lose and still be successful.

It's great for parents to be involved, instead of simply dropping kids off, picking them up and expecting their team to be a babysitting service in between. Not everyone is qualified to coach, but everyone can be supportive, yet responsible. Taking time to watch practices and be at games, even if your child isn't the star, is a great way of showing them you care. Summertime is a great opportunity for outdoor activities, and mixing sports and kids can be a great way to get some exercise and have some family fun.[59]

That's why when I was little, my mother often told us kids to go outside and play. I don't remember refusing her very often because who didn't like playing? I know she wasn't trying to get rid of us; she was simply encouraging us to get some exercise and enjoy playing with the neighbor kids.

In my hometown, summer playtime included games of kick the can, all-day pickup baseball games, exploring the nearby woods and even just sitting around to pass the time.[60] As a parent, summer is a great time for fun competitions, too. Whether it's golfing with your friends in a scramble while raising money for charity, or playing Ladder Toss in a friendly backyard game, summer is the time to have some rest and relaxation. Family fun might include water balloons on a hot day, staring games at dinner, thumb wrestling before bed or a friendly board game with the clan.

As a youngster, I always looked forward to going to the county fair with my family, where there was always an opportunity to spend some money on games. Knocking over three milk bottles to win a prize brought hours of fun one summer for my brother and I as we won over twenty new Major League Baseball replica batting helmets. Family or church picnics were also the time and place for watermelon seed- and cherry pit-spitting contests. Sure, you'd get a little messy, but nothing like turning a little garbage into a contest. In fact, certain candy can create some good spit and…well, you get the picture.

Company picnics were good for a friendly game of pick-up softball, with parents and kids playing side-by-side, working off the scrumptious picnic lunch of hamburgers, potato salad and baked beans. We've also heard of the cow pie toss, and I understand the record for the longest burp is over 18 seconds. There are towns that host annual events for yodeling, telling the best fish story, or betting on a rubber duck to float fastest down a river. Our imagination is the only limit we have when it comes to summer fun. The basis for these contests is that everyone tries to win, but no one gives a rip if you lose. The only "requirement" is that you walk away with a big smile on your face because you had fun and maybe you even made a new friend. There should be no arguing and certainly no need to yell at a referee. When we can play without any pressures, we will experience a healthy peace.

New Orleans Pelicans NBA scout Ron Meikle commented how lucky he felt to be able to grow up on a farm in Wisconsin, where he learned how to work and enjoy life as a child. "I used to get to school early, so we could play full-court basketball outside," Meikle said. "Oh, we had so much fun. Now, do you think kids do that? Are you kidding me?"

Meikle went on to tell how he started playing basketball in the fourth grade, and for his 10th birthday party, his mom invited ten of his friends over for the special event. They were each asked to bring a dollar, to be used towards the purchase of Meikle's present. They went to the local sporting goods store to buy a basketball for $8.95, which had Gus Johnson, Meikle's favorite player's name, on the ball. The store owner pumped it up for them, gave them a couple of patches for potential holes down the road, and they headed home to play the rest of the day in Meikle's barn on the cement court Ron's dad helped create by making sure the haymow was out of the way. Because of those precious memories, Meikle was able to recount that wonderful experience from so many years ago. That's the way it should be for all kids.

Over the years, I've spoken to people who feel the sooner we get our kids used to the pressures of life through sports, the better off they'll be. Honestly, I believe the sooner we get our kids used to the pressures of life, the sooner they'll become an adult. So, let's not rush our kids to adulthood. It'll happen soon enough, and all of us need time to let our hair down, so to speak. Positively having fun with friends or with family, is a great way to relax. Harmful fun at the expense of others is the life of a fool. As long as our desire for fun is pointed in the right direction, and doesn't cause us to lower our standards of character, all of these activities contribute to a fun-filled day – and that's just in the summer.[61]

In winter, we would dig tunnels in the snow drifts, have snowball fights, and of course, go sledding. Even cross-country skiing became a great activity when we got older. Those were the days, and we sure had a lot of fun.

That's what "play" is meant to be – fun! Humans are designed by nature to play and it's not something that's supposed to end after childhood. It's also something that's not supposed to be taken away from childhood. Webster's Dictionary defines "play" as a way to occupy oneself in recreation, amusement or sport. Many kids surely take part in the sport aspect of this, and that's why sports can be such a great way to play. With sports leagues starting at earlier ages than when I was young, we must be careful to keep these activities fun.

If you are looking for a chance to catch a peak at all the rookies and have nothing but fun doing it, put the pros aside and check out your local T-Ball league. There's nothing better for unadulterated excitement than watching youngsters begin their baseball journey. From what I experienced as a parent, opening night for T-Ball usually consisted of several stations, which included some form of throwing, catching, running, and hitting. Volunteers, which consisted of either parents or local varsity baseball players, scribbled numbers on charts to evaluate youngsters, so balanced teams could be formed, so any coach would be willing to oversee any of the teams. Constant rotating got everyone graded, and no stacked teams were allowed.

Is there anything more fun than watching a beginner with a tongue sticking out of the corner of his or her mouth trying to remember with which foot to lead when making a throw? As the toss was completed, you heard, "Good job Billy," and the tongue went back in the mouth and the best part reappeared – the smile.

"Did I do good?" "You sure did Billy." Confidently pounding his glove, the little boy moved on with sheer delight.

The second night of T-Ball was when the brightly colored shirts with the printed names of sponsors from the local meat market, grocery store or lumberyard were dispersed, and everyone found out who was on which team. There may have been some initial disappointment because certain friends weren't on the same team, but that quickly disappeared as the pride of their new "uniform" and team quickly took over.

What made T-Ball so popular that President Ronald Reagan hosted a game on the South Lawn of the White House? T-Ball is a great way to introduce baseball to our kids, teach them basic skills and have fun. There should be no pressure, and everyone gets along. It's easy to coach a T-Ball team on which more attention should be dedicated to teaching kids to drop the bat instead of throwing it, running to first base instead of third after a clean hit, or rotating boys and girls defensively so everyone gets a chance to play their favorite position. When you make the game fun, kids will look up to you for a long time.

T-Ball is an opportunity for parents to develop proper sportsmanship habits right from the beginning. In fact, there's only a couple you really need to perfect – smiling and giving the thumbs-up signal. As a T-Ball game concludes, the kids happily look for a treat at the concession stand. They can't wait for next week, and the only thing that should be hurting is your cheeks after so much pleasure.[62]

When NFL analyst Cris Collinsworth was interviewed for a "Playbook for Parenting" article, he commented that many adults put pressure on their children by turning sports into work. Collinsworth said he frequently spoke with his kids but tried not to force-feed them. It seems to me force-feeding is a common mistake. We seem to be compelled to have structure in our kids' lives – to schedule their fun. In my opinion, that's about as possible as scheduling quality time with our kids, because we can't guarantee when those special moments will come. Availability and time provide these opportunities. Scott Venci commented, "Sports at the youth levels are really supposed to be fun. It's not supposed to be about parents living through their child to get their own satisfaction." Paul Ihlenfeldt commented how he taught the kids he coached to be competitive and how to compete, but he also reminded his players that at that age, it's just a game. "It's not life or death, and it's not about making a living at it."

I think sometimes we're too worried about idle time developing into trouble. When kids have time for unadulterated play, just to have fun, it's amazing what benefits they'll experience and be able to use as they grow to become adults, and perhaps ultimately parents.

Just think of the social skills people learn when they have freedom to express themselves through unadulterated play. If kids aren't allowed to play, they will have challenges developing skills of communicating trust and pleasure and will miss out on learning how to calm and relax our nervous system so we feel safe.

I can't even count the number of times my brother and I would dream up different games in our yard, no matter what the season. Has anyone else purposely shoveled all of their snow *onto* the patio so there'd be more padding for a competitive game of tackle basketball? Not having everything dictated to us led to discovery and creativity. While experimenting in play, we knew we got our blood healthfully pumping, but the laughs we experienced certainly boosted all physical benefits of playing outside in the fresh, winter air.

Amazingly, we didn't even realize the neighborhood football games promoted bonding and a sense of community. You can't get that when we're constantly plopped and overstimulated in front of a television, laptop, or gaming screen.

Think of the perseverance we developed while playing pickup basketball games at the local YMCA for three hours on a Saturday morning. I also know when I'm done hoofing it a few miles with my dog, my back feels looser, my approach to that day is more positive, and the dog feels better, too. Play is such a good thing for kids of all ages.

As adults, other forms of playtime may come in the form of working out, playing cards, going to movies, or watching our kids recreate. Regardless, playing on a daily basis is one lesson we must remember.[63]

In Debbie Lantz's book, "I Just Want to Play," she stated, "While winning has value, it is not the only reason for youth sports programs. If play is simply reduced to notching up a win for the parent's sake, then we are likely missing our kids' perspective and the valuable benefits of play – for them. Our kids' involvement in athletic activity should be a positive, formative, and memorable experience that helps shape their desire to stay physically active and healthy throughout their lives." Former NBA player and coach Avery Johnson said this book reminds us youth sports is a great way for parents and coaches to allow children to enjoy sports without experiencing "real world" pressures. Kids should be free to be kids. No pressure. Just play.[64]

That can certainly be difficult when we understand it's news to no one that today's families are busy. In many instances, both parents work outside the home, and during off hours, the adults spend their time running from one errand or event to the next. Children have their homework and sports and other extracurricular activities. Add church activities and try to count the hours left to spend as a family. It's easy to see how the family evening meal has all but disappeared.

The truth is, the average American family is stressed, and it's time to take a deep breath and answer some vital questions. Is our family too busy? If it is, why? What can be eliminated? Parents need to make some hard choices for the sake of the family, and if they don't, the developing pressure will carry over into all the family activities and nobody will be able to relax and enjoy any of them. This is especially true for kids who are pushed and pulled from one activity to the next, rarely having downtime to relieve the pressure. It's a shame, because the reason they're supposedly doing the activities is to have fun. That pressure may be why so many kids are quitting sports at such early ages, which amazes me because they're giving up sports before they really get going, before they really understand what the games are all about. Tim Bannon reflected, "Studies have shown, especially among basketball players, and NBA observers have noticed too, how kids have played so much basketball by the time they get to college, they are just worn out. They're damaged goods." Why does this happen?

First, many kids are forced to specialize and pick one sport. Sometimes, this occurs when families are trying to simplify their lives – but in reality, end up complicating things more. Sometimes it's the coaches who feel year-round practice and commitment leads to better results. These coaches insist that kids work on one sport, even after their regular season is finished, making the seasons seem year-round. It's unfortunate because this prevents physical, mental, and emotional recuperation. Even professional sports have an off-season. When there's no down time for a kid, he or she gets burned out, leading to injuries and boredom on the field, and frustration at home.[65]

Why is this trend taking place in youth sports, where many kids are specializing and training year-round in one sport at an early age? When I was younger, multi-sport athletes seemed to be the norm and were envied by little kids who wanted to be as good as those high school athletes who excelled in several sports. In fact, one athlete from my hometown was invited to a Dallas Cowboys free-agent tryout after his college basketball career, because his high school athletic days not only included basketball, but football, baseball, and track. The Cowboys were looking for well-rounded athletes, similar to when they pursued Bob Hayes in the 1960's; he was a world-class sprinter before becoming a deep-threat wide receiver for the Cowboys.

With tournaments being conducted on a year-round basis, for about everything but football, it's easier to pick one sport, but also easier to burn out. Ron Meikle offered that AAU basketball was initially created to allow players to play more games, to improve and become better. However, now Meikle observes how the AAU environment has become a breeding ground for bad habits, and totally negates what's taught in high school or at camps, where sound fundamental drills are taught and repeated at station after station. In years past, camps were the means to exposure, in a great setting day after day as long as the camp lasted.

Honestly, I feel sorry for kids today who only play one sport, because I can't imagine my past without any of the four high school sports in which I participated. As a quarterback, I strategized with my teammates in the huddle about how we would attack the defense. In varsity basketball, I was able to lead the conference in scoring for one week and loved serving my teammates as a point guard. Baseball gave me the thrill of throwing a no-hitter and leading the conference in batting average as a senior, and the golf team furnished free golf, which can't be beat!

Of course, there are legitimate reasons some kids play only one sport: lack of time, limited budgets, needs at home or for the family business, hectic schedules, etc. However, there is one reason that emotionally challenges me and that's when coaches and/or obsessive parents force kids to pick one sport for their own selfish reasons.

I believe these following stories exemplify unacceptable, but true, stories for picking one sport.

- A brand-new varsity baseball coach was ecstatic his preseason meeting yielded twenty-five sign-ups. In fact, he was so elated, he told an opposing coach about his recruiting success. When their two teams met during the regular season, the opposing coach noticed the rookie coach only had twelve players available for that day's game. Asked to explain his low turnout, the bewildered rookie coach indicated the school's basketball coach got a hold of his hoopsters that wanted to play baseball, too, and told them if they wanted to be part of the school's basketball program, they were going to have to work on basketball year-round. With that demand, the baseball coach lost half of his players.

- A multi-sport athlete was a pro prospect as a baseball player. Instead of being supportive of the athlete, his football coach told him if he wanted to be on the football team the next year, he would have to forego summer Legion baseball. To the player's credit, he decided to ignore his football coach's demands, and baseball ultimately became his profession. Why do coaches have to make these demands? Our kids' days of fun go by so quickly anyway.

- Finally, one obsessive father didn't make it into professional football himself, so when he had a son, the father was determined to get his boy into the NFL. At age 10, the poor kid was forced to specialize in year-round football training, which included daily workouts consisting of multiple hours of drill work. I'm sure the boy liked football, but those are unrealistic expectations for a ten-year-old body to take. I wonder if he continued to enjoy playing as much as his dad enjoyed drilling him.

Why are there coaches and parents who do this? Is it pure selfishness? Is it because school administrators are pressuring coaches to win at all costs? Is it the elusive scholarship, or glamour and glory for parents? Regardless of the real reason, this era of specialization comes with a price. With a high level of competition year-round, not only are kids burning out mentally, they are burning out physically. Dr. James Andrews, the nationally renowned orthopedic surgeon, has said overuse injuries are much more prevalent in youth sports than they were in the days of multi-sport athletes. He has also stated more kids are having surgery for chronic sports injuries. The pressure on our kids to be able to go to school for free, and/or pursue amazing salaries in professional sports, is turning sports activities to be more like work than the fun that was intended with their creation.

Because of advancements with some surgeries, such as the Tommy John procedure, the allure for large salaries has even encouraged kids to take some extra physical risks. For those that may not know, this is typically a baseball-related procedure that repairs a torn ligament in the arm. Advancements in surgical technique have produced incredible results, where quite often it is felt the arm is better and stronger after the surgery than before. Therefore, some young athletes try to injure themselves so they can have the surgery and try to improve their chances of making it to levels they didn't think they could reach under normal circumstances. Unfortunately, this mindset is all about pursuing sports for the wrong reason – and it isn't for fun.

Playing multiple sports gives our body the opportunity to use certain muscles while others are resting. By forcing kids to pick one sport, the same muscles are used repeatedly without recovery time. Why can't one sport serve as a training program for another? Yes, professional athletes focus on one sport, but even they adjust their off-season training to allow for complete recovery.[66]

A major college assistant basketball coach told me if kids are good enough in their respective sport, coaches would know about them. He went on to say, kids don't have to play on AAU teams to be noticed. Yet the growth of club sports teams continues. The fallout on the high schools from the growth of clubs can be seen across the sports landscape. Coaches and players are burning out. Athletes are suffering the overuse injuries, and schools are losing their two- and three-sport stars to specialization. Students transfer because of their win-at-all-cost approach and club ties.

Colleges also help diminish the value of high school athletics by recruiting mostly from the club ranks, so I get how attending a weekend tournament can allow for visibility of a higher volume of talented players. The point we need to remember is that high schools still offer an all-around experience that clubs can't provide. From what I understand, the United States is the only country in the world that offers sports through its school systems. Every other country has clubs where only the elite athletes or the wealthy can compete. Is that what we want?[67]

Jackie Robinson was one of the greatest athletes of all time, yet many only know him as a baseball player. While attending UCLA, Jackie starred in football, basketball, track, and baseball. I'm glad he wasn't forced to pick one sport at an early age, because reportedly, baseball was his least favorite sport – the very sport where he made history as the first African American to break the color barrier in Major League Baseball.

The other reason kids are dropping out of sports at a young age is due to the fact there are parents who are trying to live vicariously through their kids. Their intentions may be good, but their "support" mounts tremendous pressure on the kids. Parents try to emulate professional coaches in the name of bettering their kids' skills, and the game becomes all about winning. Is it enjoyable to have to be the best, to have to win all the time, to have to take the sport seriously every minute to show your commitment? Is it enjoyable for adults when their boss at work is that demanding? Walls of resentment are built that are hard to break through, and the next thing you know, the child wants to quit. Parents need to think about sports from the child's perspective. The motivation for kids playing sports should be enjoyment, making friends and learning valuable lessons. When the stress levels get too high at home, parents should ask themselves if their children are playing competitive sports for the right reasons. Are they playing in the right type of league? Does the philosophy of the coach match that of the family's? How often will they practice? How much will each child play? How important is winning to the coach?

When parents get all the right information, they can make better decisions – decisions that will determine whether sports have become too much. Keeping youth sports in perspective will allow families to be families again, and to have fun doing it.

Here's a story about how to keep sports in the proper perspective – to have fun.

Picture some of the best young high school basketball players facing off in an AAU tournament. Boys on teams from all over the state are intensely competing at a huge athletic facility that seems to go on for miles. Also, imagine that at the same time in the very same facility, a Special Olympics soccer event is being conducted. High-level basketball games on one side of the facility and special soccer athletes with a high-level of energy on the other side. Also, imagine the two events being represented by completely different behavior sets.

On the one side of the facility, families are giving officials a hard time about calls made and missed – acting as if lives will be affected by the outcome of these games. On the other side of the facility, parents and fans are cheering for everyone and players are encouraging each other whether they are winning or losing. What matters here is playing hard and having fun. Can you tell who's playing on what side? You get one guess.

Imagine that as the day progresses, some of the basketball players sit down and watch a little soccer. Picture how the boys smile and notice how much the soccer players are enjoying their game. Fancy that the basketball boys begin to cheer the soccer players on and even converse with them between games. Visualize how the basketball players realize how blessed they are, when they comment, "We could watch them play soccer all day. This is really cool!"

Some of the parents from both venues intermingle and share their feelings. The soccer players' parents are elated that their sons or daughters have something in which to partake. They don't care about winning or losing, but participation and friendship. These parents aren't concerned about impressing some college scout, but helping their child enjoy the moment.

On this day, true sportsmanship was on display on one side of the big gym, and a work in progress on the other side. When we have the proper perspective, live for the moment, and aren't concerned about future gain, games are fun. This anecdote doesn't have to be an anomaly, it can be the norm. I'm not imagining that, because I believe it.[68]

You may say I'm a dreamer, but I'm not the only one. I hope someday you'll join us, and the world will live as one...
            – John Lennon – "Imagine" – 1971.

Chapter 11

Parental Support

What do these things have in common?

Air so fresh it almost hurts to breath; flapping wings from Canada geese; the roar from a string of Harley-Davidson motorcycles.

Volunteers umpiring for the love of the game; unadulterated laughter in the bleachers after a well-delivered punchline; carillon bells playing a favorite hymn at a nearby church.

Bright yellow dandelions popping up along fence lines; the lingering hint of cow manure; bursting buds on the mighty oak tree; blooming trilliums dotting the adjacent forest floor.

Teammates cheering a routine play like it was the last out of the World Series; soaring hawks searching for unsuspecting prey; the smell of cooked brats and hamburgers wafting past our noses.

Buzzing mosquitoes making their first appearance of the year; kids playing Got-It Dropped-It on the merry-go-round for hours on end; warm sunshine peeking through banks of white, billowy clouds.

Echoes of a slamming portable bathroom door; robins chirping in the flowering crab-apple trees; freshly cut grass; opponents cheering a good play; serenading red-winged blackbirds on a fence post; coaches accepting officials' judgements without delay; the sweet aroma of lilacs.

These are things we can see, hear, and smell as parents when we're relaxed and taking in a game at a ballpark or field somewhere – anywhere outside. Our senses will explode in no particular order when everyone remembers games at the park are for fun, and to be won or lost graciously.

Whether it's a weekend coed church school softball tournament, a weeknight Little League baseball game, a contest at the new soccer facility, or a weekend Pop Warner football tilt, it shouldn't matter. Parents doubling as fans need to realize their role is to have fun and enjoy a game. Whether it's with people we love or pausing down the block while out alone walking the dog, a game should be an enjoyable experience.

When a proper frame of mind consistently accompanies us to the sports fields like a folding chair in the trunk of our car, the cornucopia of tinglers will delight our senses like they do for a brand-new bear cub emerging from its den for the first time.

When stress tags along, many of the delights won't be experienced. Our vision is blurred. Our hearing is impaired. Our blood boils, so smells will be soured.

Our lives can be full of hassles, deadlines, frustrations and demands. However, youth sporting events *can* be a great place to downshift from emergency mode and leave the harmful effects on mind and body behind. Stress can be helpful when we need to be on our toes at work or school, but long-term exposure to stress can lead to serious health problems. This doesn't allow us to be the best we can be as parents, or as fans.

When I'd watch the Milwaukee Brewers play at old County Stadium, I'd eagerly look forward to walking through the section gate to get the first glimpse of the field and all its wonders. Imagine what I experienced when my dad and I walked into Game 5 of the 1982 World Series. The same thing applies at Lambeau Field in Green Bay, with the wonderful parking lot aromas and the well-manicured, radiant green playing surface.[69]

Being outside has nature to help us relax. Indoors for basketball, volleyball, wrestling, and other sports causes us to find different ways to minimize our stress. I know the smell of popcorn is a fantastic companion to a tasty treat to help us maintain our sense of order at an event. Hot dogs can do the trick, too. Nonetheless, our intention is to enjoy watching our kids, grandkids, or neighbor kids, and it should be fun, not stressful.

Nonetheless, difficult circumstances in our lives often lead to stress, and complaining and worrying is a natural response. We attempt to find the quickest way of escape, instead of finding and resolving the root cause. Some try to run and avoid confrontation altogether, allowing the situation to either fester or surface where it can be publicly embarrassing – at a youth sports event.

Unfortunately, the stress we encounter as adults often trickles down to our children. For instance, our bills might cause a family to force a child to pick one sport. Social status might cause parents to expect their children to perform at impossible levels. Even if we don't directly pressure our kids, they can tell when something is wrong. Whatever the cause of these stressful situations, we all (myself included) can do a better job of handling them. To help our children cope with stress, we should re-evaluate our expectations and let them help come up with solutions. Help them be in activities *they* enjoy.

Here are some tips on how we can diffuse our own stress:

One mistake we often make is getting worked up before we know all the facts. These are called knee-jerk reactions, and more often than not, these responses cause more trouble than solutions. When we respond in a hasty manner like this, instead of in a calm, appropriate manner, or if we assume incorrectly, we cause unnecessary grief. If we reach out to our creator for wisdom to help us through a situation, it's amazing the solutions that'll be provided to diffuse our stress.

Drinking plenty of water while we work on what we can control, is a great way for us to pause from the problems we face. In turn, we will be able to focus better on the task at hand, instead of the deadlines we may have imposed on us, or self-imposed *by* us.

Do you have your own quiet time? As I've made clear, my walks with our dog is my quiet time, and gives me a wonderful time for private meditation, which brings incredible ideas for projects, family situations, and just about anything. *Plus*, it's a great time for exercise, and peace and quiet. It's amazing how good I feel after my quiet time. I recommend it for everyone, because not only is it fun, but it also helps me develop the habit of hoping for the best in the most stressful of situations.

When we follow these simple steps, our stress will diminish and we will be more content, and so will our kids.[70] If we don't, we are jeopardizing the very avenue of comfortable release sports should be for our beloved children.

Therefore, my concern is especially for the kids' long-term emotional state. Our kids have countless opportunities, and these should be life-building experiences, helping them be awesome at what they choose to do in life. For some kids, that's happening. It is unfortunate, but there are a growing number of kids with mounds of pressure heaped on them, and they're trying to get our attention.[71] Here is a story forwarded to me exemplifying how a young boy was trying to get attention for a different reason, and how it affected a man's life forever.

A young, successful businessman was driving down a city street, going too fast in his fancy car. Watching for kids running between parked cars, he slowed down when he thought he saw something. Luckily, no children ran out.

Instead, a brick smashed into the passenger door of his car. The driver slammed on his brakes and backed up to the spot where he was sure the brick had been thrown. Jumping out of the car, the businessman grabbed the first kid he saw, pushed him up against a parked car and started ranting and raving. Trying to figure out why the boy threw the brick and informing him how much the damage would cost, the driver read the little kid the riot act.

The young boy was sorry. He pleaded he didn't know what else to do. He had attempted to get the attention of other drivers, but no one would stop and take notice. Obviously shaken, the boy began to tell of how his brother had rolled off the curb and fell out of his wheelchair. He led the driver to the spot where his brother laid and explained how he was too heavy to lift back into the chair all by himself. With tears in his eyes, the boy asked the shocked businessman if he would please help get his injured brother back into his wheelchair.

Emotionally moved, the driver quickly returned the fallen brother to his seat. Cleaning him up, he could tell he wasn't hurt badly. The boy thanked the driver repeatedly for helping his injured brother. Still distraught, the businessman could only watch as the boy pushed his brother home.

The driver slowly walked back to his sports car. The dent in his passenger door was obvious, but he never repaired it because he wanted to be reminded of the lesson he had learned: "Don't go through life so fast that someone has to throw a brick at you to get your attention!"

Kids are trying to get our attention. Parental behavior at contests, pressures to play certain sports or perform at a certain level are causing children to react in several ways. With kids quitting sports at an alarming pace, obesity and suicide rates increasing rapidly and an overall increase in childhood stress, a message is being sent.[72]

Our kids count on their support-system, and they need to know they can accomplish anything they set their minds to but will have to overcome slips and setbacks. As adults and parents, we are that support-system that needs to encourage and uplift them through tough times, providing the hope they desperately need, and the unconditional love necessary to weather these temporary challenges.[73]

I grew up in a family where we always had a dog. We were a German Shepherd family, and I fondly remember each of my pets' names and the daily joy they provided. These companions were important members of my family. It's been reported that dogs help humans live longer, so why wouldn't everyone want a dog, right? If we can't manage our own stress and the pressure we put on our kids, maybe it makes sense to enlist the help of a trusted pet.

Regardless of what's going on in our lives, they are always ready to lick your face or wag their tail to tell you how much they love you. If we were to describe our ideal human friend, we would all want someone who's a loyal, positive, great listening up-lifter, always willing to give of themselves. These characteristics could easily describe our favorite dog. As I've grown older, I realize the greatest benefit of man's best friend is they do exactly what we're discussing, and that's reducing our stress levels.

As we've mentioned, life is filled with obstacles and situations that can heap huge amounts of stress upon our shoulders. As adults, and especially when we become parents, do we become better at handling stress? Looking around at athletic events, I'm not convinced we can conclude that.

While kids turn to sports to blow off steam, as long as parents keep forcing kids into athletics on their terms instead of letting the kids play, stress will continue to exist and mount. It's okay for a child experiencing butterflies before a big game, because that helps us prepare for life. There is a warning though, because as soon as we turn every game into a big game, then kids will suffer and break down. Maybe that's why the suicide and obesity rates are higher than ever.

Kids are trying to tell us; they don't like being treated like a commodity anymore. Putting a first grader on a traveling team so they can begin preparing for their varsity season twelve years down the road is absurd. Does everything have to be organized? Does everything have to be tournament-related? What happened to the driveway time? What happened to good old-fashioned 1-on-1 or 2-on-2 games on the playground? Where have all the pick-up baseball games gone that used to be played in the back field or schoolyard with no adults present? We must stop putting unrealistic expectations on our kids and let them enjoy the journey. We must end the anointing of our children as being the next 5-star prospect or prodigy. Our children want stability, consistency, and loyalty – exactly what a dog provides. They want coaches who care enough to catch them smoking on a bridge and help them get involved in something productive. They want parents, not just their pets, who will love them unconditionally. They want a stress-free environment they can trust, like sports used to be until parents and adults, in general, goofed it up. The best part is we can fix it too, and we won't have to pretend to wag our tail like a dog.[74]

What are the results when parents can't control their stress and end up transferring it to their kids, or others? Sadly, in those situations, parents could end up ruining the fond memories of their children's youth, by not letting kids be kids.

According to a June 2020 adidas Runtastic article by Dr. Josh Axe, the stress that kids, and parents, are experiencing in life is the reason 75-90 percent of all doctor's office visits are related, either directly or indirectly, to conditions caused by stress. The article continues to say stress is a major problem in today's modern world, thanks to social media, long working hours, lack of physical activity, and other factors. Dr. Axe listed the five most common effects of stress:

- Stress Makes it Harder to Get Good Sleep. Because kids are still growing, missing out on sleep is the last thing they need.

- Stress Increases Cravings. Because stress hormones can interfere with our mood, sleep, and digestion, high stress levels commonly contribute to sugar and carbohydrate cravings.

- Stress Contributes to Digestive Disorders. Stress can increase inflammation, which can damage tissue in the gastrointestinal tract, thus interfering with proper nutrient absorption.

- Stress Makes it Difficult to Stay Active. Because stress increases inflammation and weakens the immune system, it can also contribute to lack of energy, slowed workout recovery, frequent illness, and the development of pain, soreness and/or stiffness in our muscles and joints.

- Stress can Lead to Brain-Fog, Moodiness & Low Willpower. When we are under constant stress and glucose is being diverted to address these potential threats, this leaves less energy, or fuel, for brain activity and mood stabilization.[75]

Does it make sense to rank nine-year-old basketball players? It's bad enough we're forcing freshmen in high school to specialize. With a little research, we can find other cases to show this phenomenon exists and may be growing. At one time, the Washington

Post ran a story about a ten-year-old boy who was getting attention as potentially being the next LeBron James. Even George Mason University reached out to this boy through a letter of encouragement to get good grades in school. Apparently, youth soccer has gotten into the insanity as well, as an October 2013 blog entry on socceramerica.com talked about how GotSoccer.com, "the most well-known youth soccer ranking site," concluded it needed to expand its rankings to include 9- and 10-year-old teams. Just think of the ramifications of ranking kids or teams that young. Undoubtedly, it would force some parents to start kids at an earlier age and put even more pressure on youth coaches to win their games, instead of focusing on fun and development.

What should kids in this pre-adolescent age group be concerned about? Remember, we're talking about elementary school children in the third and fourth grades. According to About.com, that's an age when children are becoming more capable of taking on household responsibilities. It is a time when they become more independent by being willing to take control of their hygiene and personal care. It also is a time when kids are becoming interested in having sleepovers with their friends and considering friendships to be very important. As they become more socially conscious, they are concerned about bettering the world and helping others. Does that sound like an age for kids to worry about where they're nationally ranked in their sport? As the soccer blog opined, it seems more like "adults competing against other adults through their children."

Attention youth sports adults: It's time to back off and let our kids be kids. Please let them play the games they love and put the rankings away![76]

All I know is when the cool air and the smell of fall leaves arrives, it reminds me of how it used to be when I was a young football player – a fond memory I cherish. In my hometown, I played for the Bears, but we weren't from Chicago. As an eighth grader, we won the championship, but it wasn't against the Packers. Youth football memories include throwing a last second touchdown pass against the Lions, to preserve our divisional lead and cement our spot in the title game. During the season, we practiced two nights a week and looked forward to our Saturday games with great anticipation. Our hearts (at least mine did) would go pitter pat as the girls from our school would walk around the field on practice nights. Sometimes, we even got to play under the lights on the same field as our town's high school heroes. How special was that? Those days seemed so pure and innocent because they were.

What could ruin something as special as that? One disturbing reality is how parents will work their way over to the sidelines and loudly enlighten the officials of their lack of quality. Once again, impressionable ears are everywhere, and inappropriate language is often being used. In the perfect world, no self-respecting parent would feel the need to do this, especially since they more than likely never officiated football themselves. Quite often, these officials at non-varsity levels are inexperienced up-and-comers, but even veteran varsity officials with extensive playoff experience are working youth games and they're being told the same thing. How embarrassing for those kids to have to deal with parents who do this. Tim Bannon offered this idea, when he said, "I think every parent of an athlete, and every athlete, too, should at some point be a ref or an umpire, because then you realize how hard it is. Not only hard to just do the job, but how hard it is to deal with parents and fans." Bannon went on to say, "I wouldn't want to be a basketball ref in a small gym." Is it any wonder quality officials are hard to find?

It's time to take a step back and take inventory of our behavior. We're ruining our kid's experience and it's going to be hard for many of today's kids to have the same fond memories they deserve when everything is taken so seriously. It's time to relax, take a deep breath and inhale the sweet aroma of youth.[77]

Another example of parents not being able to manage how stressful they make it for kids is when they try to live vicariously through their children. How many little girls will be forced to fight through chronic knee problems so they can participate in gymnastics and/or figure skating, just for the remote chance their mothers will be shown on television during a future Olympiad? I had a mother tell me that was her goal. Did you get that? *Her* goal, not her *daughter's.*

How many little boys will play on travel basketball teams because their dad wants to make sure son gets the scholarship dad didn't? With all the exposure sports receives, it's hard to keep sports in proper perspective. However, when family members begin to suffer for the sake of hollow parental glory, it's time to step back, or step in, because the focus needs to be on kids having fun and developing great habits for life.

If a good friend or family member is misguiding their children, do we have the courage to step forward in love for the sake of the child(ren) involved? When a parent chastises a child for not performing up to that parent's expectations, it's sad, but when a family shares a smile together because of the fun they had, excitement prevails.[78]

Obviously, there are an infinite number of examples of poor parental behavior, but one involved a couple who was cited for starting a brawl of about twenty adults after a youth baseball game. The ten-year-old players were crying because of the behavior demonstrated by their parents. Of course, the instigating couple felt they were the ones who were attacked. At a youth wrestling tournament, two mothers ended up exchanging fisticuffs after harsh words describing how the opposing son was wrestling their own child, and the fight took place right in front of their kids. Imagine the scar those boys could carry with them the rest of their lives.

When it comes to family matters, including youth sports, parents are the ones who are supposed to know how to best help their kids, and this is best handled with a family discussion. What are our kids' goals, and our family priorities? Are they even being considered in all of this? In spite of all the medical data supporting variety in their activities, parents continue to channel kids into one sport, and therefore setting them up for overuse injuries. We see parents carrying kids all over the place to either play on the school's team or a club team (or two) after that.

Because youth sports are such a big industry, scheduling conflicts arise between school-sponsored teams and club teams. Because of an overlap in schedules, girls were forced to choose between their high school teams in state championship games or their club team in the opening rounds of a regional championship, where more college scouts would be coming to watch. These are decisions kids shouldn't have to make. It's crazy to make high school girls choose which team they want to play with and decide which group of people they have to let down. It's a lose-lose situation. Another example of causing sports to be stressful for our kids.

Again, our country has fallen in love with tournaments. Week after week, our kids play in tournaments with sometimes three to four basketball games in a day. When setting up sports schedules, are the best interests of kids being considered, or are the parents and adults scheduling simply to generate more money? Have you ever played four basketball games in a day?

What happens when parents step back, release the stress, and let kids be creative?

On one occasion a middle-school football team decided to help their learning-disabled teammate by purposely taking a knee at the 1-yard line to allow their friend an opportunity to score the first, and perhaps only, touchdown of his life. The players planned and schemed without any of the coaches knowing what they were going to do. The resulting touchdown didn't change just one player's life, but all the lives of the players on the team. Some of them never knew how to serve another, until they helped their teammate with his successful 1-yard TD. Isn't it amazing what kids can come up with when adults (parents) aren't as involved?[79]

One great way to survive what can be a crazy sports climate, is to execute balance, which reminds me of when I was young. Back then, I climbed some pretty tall trees with huge branches that encouraged traveling from one side of the tree to the other. Rest assured, games of tag in high places can be challenging. These were trees your mother preferred you didn't climb, but when being as high as you could and looking out over your corner of the world, the feeling was that of amazing freedom. Obviously, I had some pretty good balance, or you wouldn't be reading this today.

I'm still amazed we don't hear more stories about tightrope walkers falling to their death, but of course they've gotten smarter by putting nets underneath the high wire. In sports we constantly hear coaches maintaining they need to have better balance for more team production. In football, it's about a better balance between the run and the pass. As much as the NFL has become more pass-oriented, if you aren't able to run the ball at times, the offense becomes predictable, and the defense only has to worry about rushing the passer.

In basketball, the team that's able to score from inside and out has a better chance than trying to succeed at only one facet of the game. Also, teams depending on only one player aren't well-balanced either. As soon as the star gets hurt or is having an off game, the rest of the team will have a hard time picking up the slack. They're not as likely to be prepared because they've become accustomed to rely on the one person.

Our lives can fall out of balance in a hurry also, which brings us to the story of the chair. I heard this story being told to a group of aspiring basketball players by a basketball teacher passionate about helping kids succeed not just in basketball, but most importantly in life. In order for that to happen, balance is required.

When a four-legged chair is placed on a flat surface, it's easy for someone to sit on the chair because it has great balance with all four legs properly touching the floor. Grab the chair and tilt it, and now it's not so easy to sit on, because the proper balance is lost. Each leg of the chair represents an area of our lives – faith, family, school/work, and sports. Nowadays, we're seeing too many families out of whack because of sports. When too much emphasis is put on sports, we lose our focus – our balance – and we're headed for a proverbial fall. The chair is a simple device performing an important task – when balanced. When we follow a balanced lifestyle, our lives will be simpler. When the basketball coach was done with his short little talk, the kids seemed to get it. However, would the parents? Instead of pushing our kids towards unrealistic expectations and impending discomfort, let's guide them to a balanced life of satisfaction and fun – just like climbing one of those giant trees.[80]

This story would be appropriate for parents to communicate to their children, as all communication is vital. What role do the kids need from their parents to succeed? This question needs to be asked, so parents can go the appropriate extra mile for their kids. While parents may think screaming at a contest is encouraging, it is more likely embarrassing, pushing kids into the laps of other people, who may not be the best influence. Little things, like stopping afterward for ice cream, may be the ticket to a renewed relationship. Perhaps a great listener is all that's needed.

We're all responsible for our decisions and we've all made mistakes, but there's always time to repair as long as we're apologetic and willing to change.

Stress-free living and proper parental support is the ideal result to pursue, and the best opportunity for that to take place is in a balanced, loving home.

Here are ten ways the former website essortment.com suggested to show our kids our love:

- Talk with them. Make a list of today's conversations. Cross out those that included lectures or instructions. Any left? Make time to talk without strings attached.
- Listen to them. How often do we hear them, but don't actually listen?
- Write them a note. Stick one in their books or mail them a letter.
- Play with them. For all the busyness in our lives, there is always time on the way to sports practice to play some sort of word game in the car.
- Hug them. Many kids don't get physical attention after the baby stage. Hugging our kids will not only make them feel better, but also us.
- Read to them – children who are read to tend to do better in school. For older kids, take turns reading longer stories and take time for discussions.
- Brag about them. Be supportive – emphasize the positives – especially when they are within earshot.

- Do something unusual with them. Spontaneity can produce some of the best memories.
- Include them in decisions. Allow them to help decide important things in their lives as well as the family's.
- Ask them for advice. Seeking their opinion makes them feel important – and loved.[81]

If we're going to force our kids to do anything, let's teach them fundamentals of life like proper handshakes and greetings by name while looking people in the eyes. Teaching teamwork through communication, bodily fitness through fun exercises, and the washing of hands before eating. Saying "please" and "thank you" when getting food, learning the value of fruits and vegetables, and cleaning tables and pushing in chairs after eating would be phenomenal. What about when the day ends, we return to fundamentals, by teaching our kids to show appreciation through hugs and handshakes for "forcing" them to learn some valuable basics?

I'm convinced if we spend more time teaching our kids those fundamentals of life, instead of running them around weekend after weekend from one tournament to the next like mini-professional athletes, they're going to have a better chance to make it in life, and the kids will live more stress-free with the confidence to make it big if they really want to, because as parents we'll be supporting them without fail, just like kids want and need.[82]

When Ryan Borowicz described his parents, you could tell he was thankful for the shining example they provided. "My parents certainly guided me, and they still do. I think their values and teaching the difference between right and wrong is the most overriding thing they taught me. Take that stability they've given me over my lifetime and the knowledge that there's always stability there in their faith, their work, their demeanor, and when everything about them is stable, it allows you to be creative and branch out a little bit, like traveling to other countries and trying different things." Ryan's parents were, and still are, lights in his life.

Chapter 12

Gratitude vs Entitlement

I was informed the average person will open their mouth to speak approximately 700 times a day. Drawing on my own experience, dare I say not all of those times are done well. As I continue to strive to improve, there is a simple two-word sentence I must say more often.

Many of us have held the door for someone and expected something in return for what we did. It wasn't money, but that little two-word sentence, *thank you*. It's not proper to do things for others and expect something in return. If that's our motive, we're doing things for the wrong reason. However, it is an act of common courtesy to express our gratitude when someone does something nice for *us*. We can never say *thank you* too much, so it's time for each one of us to make better use of those 700 times we speak – to improve our average.[83]

Besides, saying *thank you* to improve our average, we can also improve our health by being grateful. According to a 2018 submission to The Thrive Global Community by Carrie D. Clarke, who can be reached at www.nextlevelcoachconsult.com, the more you do it, the easier it gets. That's not just overcoming inertia, so to speak, but frequently practicing gratitude increases our dopamine production, which encourages our brains to want more of the same. As Clarke put it, "the more you are grateful for, the more you will find to be grateful for." Clarke also compiled ways to practice gratitude and those are as follows:

- Keep a gratitude journal.
- Tell an employee or a friend something you appreciate about them.

- Look at yourself in the mirror and think of something you like about yourself.
- Sit in a quiet place and think about when something went well. How did that feel? Practice that feeling every day for a week.
- Next time something bad happens, consider five good things that happened because of this event.
- Write someone a thank you note.
- Write it down, talk about it, think about it, re-live it, meditate.
- Rinse and repeat.[84]

It's also a commonly held belief that we have five traditional senses: seeing, hearing, taste, smell, and touch. To develop appreciation for our senses, sometimes it helps to temporarily eliminate them. This may include covering the ears to represent being deaf, covering the eyes to simulate blindness, etc. I've never even temporarily lost my senses, but it's said when a sense is eliminated, the others become more acute.

Years ago, when I broke my shooting-hand wrist in that summer league basketball game, I'd like to think that experience gave me a sample of what it'd be like to lose a sense, because being forced to rely on my opposite hand helped me improve in basketball – and ambidexterity – over the course of those eight healing weeks, not the least of which included writing with my opposite hand. As I mentioned, going through that injury helped me appreciate the use of two healthy hands.

Have you ever thought about which sense to give up if you had to?

I love music, so trying to imagine not enjoying all my favorite genres almost seems unimaginable. If I had no ability to hear, I would have missed the roar of the Lambeau Field faithful when Desmond Howard returned a San Francisco 49ers punt 71 yards for a touchdown only two minutes into the 1997 "Mud Bowl" playoff game. Without audio, I probably wouldn't have rejoiced as much at my wife's "I do" or the inaugural guttural laughs of my baby boys. No songbirds? No way. Therefore, it would be easier to be blind, right?

Wait a minute. Then I couldn't have been as sentimental watching my bride walk up the aisle, or as excited observing each of our boys accomplish their own unique athletic or drama successes. That includes our fourth son being part of a first-ever high school track and field team and clearing the opening height in the high jump event at the conference meet without ever practicing once, because he was a team player and followed his coach's desire to enter the event as a last minute entry in an attempt to try and get more team points. Because they were just starting out, they didn't even have high jump equipment with which to practice. Therefore, his "practice" came via watching high-jumping technique videos on the internet.

Would I be able to give up smell and miss the aroma of lilac bushes or flowering fruit trees in the spring? While attending college, the smell of the Milwaukee breweries offered an interesting aroma. Would hearing the crack of the bat on a sunny Saturday afternoon be the same without the savory odors of some of the finest tailgating in all of sports? If you can smell all that fine bratwurst, would it be as delightful if you couldn't taste it? My life certainly would've been different without being able to taste Mom's delicious orange daffodil cake she made for my birthday every year.

That leaves the sense of touch. I could've done without a few of the minor skin burns I experienced in life, including the "healthy" finger blister from melted test-tube glass after mistakenly heating a non-Pyrex test tube in a college chemistry class experiment. However, passing on touching our kids' baby-soft skin or snuggling with a cuddly pet would be tough to do.

Thankfully, my senses are intact, and I'll prayerfully be able to take in the best sights, sounds, smells, tastes and touches for a long time, because it just wouldn't be the same without all of them.[85] There are those who do not have all of their senses, yet are able to make things work just fine. As parents, setting a wonderful example of gratitude for what we physically do have, will go a long way in demonstrating to our younger family members they can be thankful, too.

Wikipedia tells us "Gratitude, appreciation, or thankfulness is a positive emotion or attitude in acknowledgment of a benefit one has received or will receive." Are we grateful for what we've been given, or are we always thinking about what we don't have?

Dissatisfaction comes when we lose that positive focus. Schools willing to start a football program for the first time; communities with iconic coaches who seemingly have been around for generations, youth programs for just about every sport; new field houses, aquatic centers and weight rooms all provide incredible opportunities for thankfulness. Today's student-athlete just about has it all, as many high schools boast the appearance of small colleges. Nonetheless, when we are thankful daily, our attitude toward life will change. We will be more positive, gracious, loving, and humble. Only being thankful at times of celebrations or big moments, when we get our way or when things are new, will cause us to take items for granted and never be satisfied or content.

Even though it is renovated, Lambeau Field, the home of the Green Bay Packers is an example of how something old can be revered throughout sports because it is a testament to eras gone by. We can never thank administrators, parents, fans, coaches, opponents and even officials enough, and as parents, we should be leading the way and setting that example. Without those involved, sporting events wouldn't be possible.

We should also be thankful for challenging times because of the good that can be accomplished through distress, but sometimes we get so wrapped up in what we don't have and miss opportunities to be grateful.

Being thankful is something that will be noticed by others if we are truly appreciative. To display that attitude of gratitude, start by remembering what we have. So often, it's easier to identify what we don't have and be a salty, snarly, *un*grateful person. Instead, we need to look around and notice the blessings we do have. My dad was very good at being appreciative of all the good things in his life. Honestly, he grew up in humble surroundings, but he didn't complain much about his upbringing, and I noticed. As parents, it's our job to pass these good habits along, so we need to help our kids understand they may not always get what they want, but they may get what they need. Which is better?[86]

As first graders, we are encouraged to bring in things for "show and tell." That exercise was a way for us to show a really cool toy, while learning to public speak for the first time. My Marquette University basketball jersey is one of my prized possessions because of the opportunities and experiences that came with it. While being a part of that program, I experienced my first jet rides, just to name one benefit. It also represents a time in my life when I stretched myself and pursued a goal for which I was told I had "no chance." Showing it to my kids hopefully helps them appreciate the wonderful experiences they've had in their lives, but also gives them the comfort to pursue their own stretch goals.

We also must remember, to whom much is given, much is expected. As thankful recipients, why not offer gifts of time, talents, and treasures to situations in your lives. It's a benefit to all of us, to teach our children that grateful people give back – they pay it forward, right? Humble, thankful people will anonymously give back, so just because we don't hear about it, doesn't mean it isn't happening.

Like many of the other character traits we've discussed, thankfulness is a habit. Do you have the attitude of gratitude?

For parents who may not have had the opportunity to be part of an athletic team, and for those who did, I need to take this time to point out what it means to be part of an athletic team, and there is one letter to start the conversation – the letter "P".

"P" stands for "Privilege".

It is a privilege for student athletes to be part of their school's sports teams. It is not a right. A privilege is a special permission or benefit granted to or enjoyed by someone. It is a privilege to be able to put on the uniform of our kids' school and to represent not only their school, but often an entire community. Those students represent their families and themselves. Notice where the word "themselves" landed in the sequence of entities represented. It was last. Let's all say it together, *there is no "I" in team.*

Scott Venci observed, "Whether parents think their kid is D-III or D-I, the amount of money and the amount of traveling leads to pressure placed on the shoulders of the kid, because now the parents want a return on their investment." This is not an environment of gratitude, but one of entitlement, which isn't conducive to good sportsmanship.

This me-first attitude was well illustrated in one scene in the movie "Miracle", which was the film telling the story about the 1980 United States Men's Olympic Hockey team – an extreme underdog that beat the vaunted Soviet Union. It was the story about how coach Herb Brooks molded and shaped a group of players from numerous schools and programs into a well-oiled, unselfish unit. He was their leader – their parent – during that training time together leading up to, and including, the Olympic Games. During the movie, Coach Brooks repeatedly asks players their names, and where they were from. The typical answer was for them to proudly proclaim their name and the college they represented. Because different members of the Olympic team were part of some intense college rivalries, up to this point proclaiming these two pieces of information was a pride issue and preventing the individual players from becoming the best they could be as one unified team. This simple question later played a significant role in his development of the meaning of "privilege".

In one pre-Olympic exhibition, Brooks caught his players talking during the game about the girls in the stands instead of focusing on the task at hand. This cost the team in a big way. After the game, Brooks forced the players to repeatedly skate wind sprints. It turned out, he was so angry, it almost seemed like he wanted to skate them right through the ice.

After what seemed like hours, one of the players blurted out his name, and Coach Brooks asked him for whom he played, and he yelled back "the United States of America." Finally, Brooks got through to his players they weren't representing their schools or themselves – they were representing a greater cause: their country.

He convinced them the name on the front of the jersey was

more important than the name on the back. He got them to realize what a privilege it was to represent their country and they needed to put their pride aside and work for the good of their team – not for themselves.

Every student athlete who makes a sports team is representing his or her school first. The money parents spend in off-season training and camps shouldn't entitle an athlete to anything. Being the best player on a team should not guarantee a spot the following year.

Parents must remember, representing one's school is a privilege, and a student athlete's behavior, effort, and performance on and off the field of play should be the method for earning that spot every season. Hopefully, high school student-athletes and their parents will realize how much of a privilege it is to represent their school, their community, their family and themselves on and off the field.[87]

Here's a wonderful historical example of how a young man expressed gratitude in an entirely different way.

Nate Ruffin was a safety for the Marshall University Thundering Herd football team. In 1970, he had 11 interceptions in only seven games because an injured shoulder prevented him from finishing the season. Many won't know who Ruffin was, but because of his selfless acts of devotion and gratitude, Marshall's football program exists today. Therefore, NFL players like Carl Lee, Troy Brown, Ahmad Bradshaw, Randy Moss, Chad Pennington and Byron Leftwich can say they had the privilege of competing for Marshall University.

In November of that 1970 season, the football team's plane crashed at the hometown airport on a return flight from a game against East Carolina killing everyone on board, which included almost the entire team, most of the coaching staff, members of the athletic department and fan base.

Because Ruffin's injury prevented him from making the trip, he and several other injured upperclassmen and all freshmen – who were not allowed by the NCAA to play varsity sports at that time – were spared.

In the days following the crash, the university's board of governors planned to suspend the program indefinitely. Ruffin acted quickly and organized a large rally of supporters outside the board meeting to convince the governors otherwise. Ruffin was grateful for the efforts of those who went before him and the opportunity to play at Marshall. To honor his fallen comrades, he felt it was best to move forward – despite the grief that lingered over the school and community. Ruffin's selfless act paved the way for the hiring of Jack Lengyel, a compassionate coach with incredible energy who took the job no one else would touch because he "wanted to help."

In the 2006 movie "We Are Marshall," which recounts the catastrophe, Lengyel told an assistant coach it didn't matter whether they won or lost, or even how they played the game – it just mattered that they played every Saturday. Lengyel resigned after only four years, but he gave a valuable part of his life to help others heal from a tragedy. It takes a special person to start a program over from scratch.

Parents, when was the last time you went up to a coach, an official or someone involved with your kids and told them thank you? How about approaching your son or daughter's youth coach to simply shake their hand and thank them – no strings attached? Most of them surely aren't looking for any pats on the back or even recognition. They're too busy giving of themselves and loving what they're doing, just like Lengyel.

Unfortunately, we too often spend time focusing on whether our child should be in the starting lineup, if they're the scoring leader or whether a college scholarship could be coming their way in 10 or more years.[88]

Nowadays, parents are taking that improper focus and directing it to make sure they spend huge amounts of money, so they can feel their kids will have a better chance of making it big. It even leads to a feeling of entitlement, because of the money spent with travel teams to partake in countless tournaments that contribute to the youth sports industry.

Youth sports tournaments bring out a wide array of people, personalities and sometimes pageantry. Especially if they're located outside, these tournaments provide music, food, and fun. Can you beat sitting in a lawn chair, getting your fill of basketball, soccer, or baseball? There are so many different sights, sounds and smells on the street, at a park or even in a gym on a sunny weekend. At these tournaments, you'll notice colorful t-shirts with catchy key-words like Elite, Select, All-Star, Prestige, Ultimate and Classic, or phrases like Tournament of Champions, State Champions and National Champions. I've seen these t-shirts apply to just about every sport.

It struck me as odd that so many kids can be part of so many superlative programs and activities. Is it possible for so many to be part of something that theoretically is supposed to be for so few? It's true, kids have more options than prior generations, but are all these "Elite" programs simply money-making ventures? Are all of these kids really that great?

I think it's awesome that kids who are serious about their athletic futures have the opportunity to get professional help to become the best they can be. However, let's remember, everyone is given a cer-tain set of talents, and upon completing these programs it's possible our kids still may not be good enough to be included in the Select, regardless of the cost and sacrifice.

Speaking of sacrifice, let's talk about the injury factor. At a tournament where we watched our oldest sons, I spoke to another mother whose eighth-grade daughter just got back into sports after an 18-month rest from overuse injuries to her knees. To make it clear, that means her body started to break down while in sixth grade. Overuse injuries are supposed to happen to 50-something year old fathers who throw extra batting practice on a Saturday morning. Again, are our kids becoming victims of an incredible business plan, incredible opportunities, or a lack of being content?

Are we a society low in self-esteem and trying to regain it through our kids?

In Pixar's movie "The Incredibles," Mr. Incredible's arch nem-esis Syndrome makes it clear he's going to send his robot off to some major city and cause severe destruction. His plan then calls for him to save the day, unlike any other superhero ever did. He emphatically states, "I'll give them heroics, I'll give them the most spectacular heroics anyone has ever seen. And when I'm old and I've had my fun, I'll sell my inventions so that everyone can be superheroes – everyone can be super. And when everyone's super" – he laughs cynically – "no one will be."[89]

Parents should be knowledgeable enough to know when modest gratitude has disappeared and the improper perspective of living vicariously through our kids' lives has taken control.

Sadly, everything could be perfectly played within the AAU system, and reaching the professional leagues or college athletics still wouldn't be a guarantee. Large sums of money and hours of practice can put one on the path to success, however success is never guaranteed, nor entitled.

For instance, let's say Billy was introduced to hockey at age 6. Because he was not from a hockey family, he took a few lessons. He loved playing and quickly learned the game. Based on Billy's enthusiasm, it was no surprise he dreamed of playing in the NHL. Even if he never made it, his parents wanted to give him a chance. Costs were high, but his parents jumped right in. Second thoughts never surfaced, and they did whatever it took, even if it meant side jobs. Billy quickly rose through the ranks of youth hockey to the AAA level, which is a stepping-stone for those who want to pursue hockey at the junior, college, and professional levels. Members of these teams compete in some of the premier tournaments, where scouts represent prep schools, junior and college hockey programs from both Canada and the United States. Billy's play at the AAA level earned him an opportunity to play juniors. For a youth hockey player aged 16-20, juniors is one step away from a college scholarship.

Juniors started a chapter of his life living away from home three-quarters of the school year and took him to cities like Detroit, Toronto, Springfield (Illinois) and Traverse City (Michigan). Host families, coaches, and his hometown high school guidance counselor would be important to Billy's academic and athletic success. Billy's family, especially his little brother, missed him tremendously, but he was focused on his dream. They attended as many games as possible, but it was hard not being there daily. Division I scholarship offers trickled in, but they weren't what Billy had hoped for. Was Billy doing everything necessary? He had received such high praise as he progressed. Were his coaches talking him up?

During his final year of juniors, Billy suffered an injury, forcing him to miss part of the season. Just like that, the scholarship offers disappeared. Time had flown by. The love of the game, strong family support and maturation beyond his years helped Billy pursue a dream. He turned out to be a great kid. Proper perspective ensured enjoyment along the way. This was a family who did everything right, especially being grateful for the journey they pursued. However, their proper perspective was the only guarantee of the situation.[90] More often than not, the failure of Billy would have meant family chaos, because families like that aren't able to be as grateful on a daily basis.

At least one day helps us remember to be thankful. It's true, we annually celebrate Thanksgiving, which reminds us all about the importance of being grateful. However, should we only be thankful one day of the year?

In the movie "Kung Fu Panda", Master Oogway told Po, the Dragon Warrior, "Yesterday is history, tomorrow is a mystery and today is a gift – that's why it's called the present." These are great ways to express how we should be thankful for every waking opportunity, and I feel sorry for anyone who has trouble getting up to start his or her day for work, school, or play.

Two-a-day practices? All right! Games on back-to-back nights? Sign me up! Financial issues? There's always hope. What do you do when something unsuspectingly breaks on your vehicle, and you have no idea how you're going to pay until someone volunteers to relieve your debt? Not only do you say thank you, but also you tell others how generous people can be. Then you give back by offering your gifts of self, time and resources to others. After success carrying the football, running backs quite often express thanks by raving about their offensive line creating big holes.

Again, should we be thankful only for celebrations?[91] Remember when gratefulness becomes an integral part of our lives, we will find our attitude change, as we become more positive, gracious, loving, and humble.

It boils down to the fact if we are truly thankful, our lives will show it. Are we thankful our kids return home safely from school? Do we take it for granted we live comfortably in a climate-controlled home? Do we thankfully choose to live in moderation, so we can help others with less? Do we show our appreciation of freedom by voting in every election?[92] Practicing these habits at sporting events and in life will naturally pass it on to our kids – daily.

Chapter 13

Grace, Forgiveness, and Compassion

There are some things glaringly missing from sports in our world today: grace, forgiveness, and compassion.

I remember a phone conversation with my late father about the wonders of the Internet and modern technology, in general. He grew up in a time when television was just beginning, and personal computers and the internet weren't invented yet during his working days. He marveled when I told him how one of his grandsons would watch his alma mater's small college football games on his laptop through the Internet's live feed as provided by the host university, while also enjoying the comfort of his bed hundreds of miles away. Arguably, my son had as good a "seat" as anyone at the game.

My dad was also amazed when we discussed smartphones. He never ended up having a cell phone, not even a flip phone, only a cordless landline. When I described what smart phones could do, I could tell he was in awe. I could detect on the other end of our call, another tone of disbelief when I described how a smartphone could contain musical playlists.

For a fan of Benny Goodman, Glenn Miller, and other big bands of the 1940's, to be able to create playlists on your phone and take them everywhere you go was an incredible concept for someone who loved music, like I do. For me, playlists are music therapy at various times during my week. As I listen to some of the songs from the '80s, I imagine the dancing on old MTV videos, or perhaps what might happen if I let the rhythm move me. For my dad's generation, the dancers of significance were none other than Fred Astaire and Ginger Rogers. For my generation, Michael Jackson was the man. As talented as Michael was, when you watched Fred and Ginger, the word 'grace' quickly came to mind, describing the well-coordinated choreography displayed in their movies.

Athletes can also be identified as graceful, but grace has other definitions referring to consideration and care for others, and expressions of kindness and mercy. Again, to show grace is to be nice to someone who doesn't deserve it. It's when favor is being extended to someone out of the goodness of the giver's heart.

You probably don't hear too many players approaching their coaches and asking for grace. They ask for some slack or another chance, but grace? Not likely. What is grace?

Grace can be used to describe a coordinated athlete or wonderful dancer, someone with good manners and considerate of others or demonstrated by way of various expressions of kindness and mercy. To show grace is to extend favor or kindness to another who may not deserve it.[93]

For instance, a team is down by several touchdowns, but the quarterback breaks through a couple of tackles and can get to the second level of the defense. He makes a move and runs the length of the football field to score. The quarterback was able to pull away from several defenders, and his teammates – instead of hustling downfield for additional potential blocking – stood back and watched the play to soak up the wonderful event that just occurred.

Parents and fans were ecstatic about the play, but should the coach lay into most of his players for not completing the play, or is this the time he gives them grace and focuses on the end result, because the touchdown was exactly what the team needed at that point in the game? In this example, the coach chose to publicly blast his players for not finishing the play and consequently, his team's life was sucked right out of them. Now they felt nothing would please him.

The coach decided praise wasn't deserved at that time, even though grace may have been more appropriate. Perhaps game film studied a couple of days later would have been a more timely opportunity for following up in a calm, teachable manner.

Immediately reacting is also a choice many parents choose to make, instead of waiting to cool down after an event, before addressing a teachable situation. In the scenario, the team that came up with the big play was behind by quite a few points, and as we see so often, a big play can immediately swing the momentum. Unfortunately, as this coach did, we as parents often squash the momentum boost our kids can use, and instead of being a great listener and an encourager for longtime benefit, they choose to be critical of minor details.

Quite often, grace is not chosen as a method of communication because it is viewed as weak and timid, because it's undeserved for the recipient. However, there is a time and place for reprimand or scolding, and a time and place for grace. When grace is delivered, favor is being extended simply out of the goodness of the heart of the giver.

Another coach observed his kicker produce less than stellar results after two first-quarter kickoffs. Instead of publicly humiliating him, he simply replaced the kicker for a couple of opportunities and then quietly reinserted him after the starter watched his replacement perform admirably.

The substitution sent the desired message without a word and accomplished the coach's mission. The grace bestowed on the kicker by quietly reinserting him thereafter produced wonderful results with back-to-back touchbacks. Having faith in our kids and giving the benefit of a second chance is a great way to build them up, and as parents, this is a great way to infuse confidence in our kids, even though they made a mistake.

Grace is free and doesn't have to be paid back. It should come with no strings attached. It is the act of unmerited favor – most often to the one who least deserves it, but also probably to the one who most needs it. As a society, are we trending more and more toward blackballing people who make mistakes? Are we a forgiving lot? Will we give people a second chance? The greatest of us are those who serve. The hand of power reaches up, while the hand of grace reaches down.[94]

The late theologian and writer Dr. Donald Barnhouse stated, "Love that goes upward is worship; love that goes outward is affection; love that stoops is grace." Do our kids have teammates who don't carry their weight? As parents, we need to speak kindly about them anyway. Are there colleagues at your workplace who complain about everything? Show them grace anyway. Do family members upset you with their decision-making? Love them anyway. In our world of give and take, rules and regulations, requirements and expectations, grace can be something that transforms lives. It's a gift we can give that's stronger than revenge, racism or hate. Grace is about tolerance, acceptance, love, warmth, and compassion. As parents, we have the choice to extend grace on a daily basis to those around us. When we do, it will give us a feeling like that music therapy flowing in our ears.[95]

When the Chicago Cubs won the 2016 World Series over the Cleveland Indians 4-3, it was their first World Series championship since 1908. Until then, they hadn't even been to the World Series since 1945. That was a lot of frustration for one team and its fan base. Cubs Nation got a taste of success when it advanced to the 2015 National League Championship Series but lost to the New York Mets in four straight games. The Cubs also made it to the NLCS in 1984, 1989 and 2003, but that's the closest they had gotten to the World Series since the '45 challenge, when they lost to the Detroit Tigers in seven games.

One could say the closest they had gotten was 2003, when in Game 6 with a 3-0 lead, a pop-up foul headed toward the stands where left fielder Moises Alou maneuvered to stretch and catch it for the second out of the 8th inning. Unfortunately, that's when Steve Bartman became part of Cubs folklore. I believe in every stadium; fans are instructed not to interfere with what takes place on the field of play. However, that's exactly what Bartman did, as he reached for the same popup Alou was trying to catch and Bartman's efforts caused Alou to miss – extending the Florida Marlins player's at-bat – seemingly causing the momentum to immediately shift. The Marlins came from behind to win Game 6 and they also won Game 7 to advance to the World Series. A self-professed die-hard Cubs fan, Bartman felt terrible and publicly apologized.[96]

When someone is offensive, rude or disrespectful towards

another, the offender needs to make it right with that person as soon as possible. They need to reflect on what they've done, vow to make a change and apologize for the hurt they've caused. For kids or parents, it's hard to humble oneself and look the person – or people – who's probably mad at you, in the eye, and say you're sorry. Nonetheless, it's the right thing to do.

In the heat of battle, when athletes or coaches cross the line and emotionally gesture or verbalize obscenities, or when parents in the stands allow their emotions to boil over, it's not okay to simply brush off the situation without making things right. It's the right thing to do even if we feel we've been offended first, because it takes a bigger person to take the lead when resolving a conflict. Unfortunately, it seems we're approaching a point where our society thinks it's okay to explode during the heat of the moment at an athletic event. It shouldn't matter if an incident occurs during an emotional game or not. Sadly, people may refer to these confrontations as amusing or entertaining. I remember jokes being made about how people used to go see "the fights" and a hockey game would break out. When that's our attitude, we have work to do.[97]

Steve Bartman even called for Cubs fans everywhere to redirect their negative feelings away from him, his family and friends and back to positive support for the Cubs. Can you imagine, *loyal* fans taking it out on one of their own? Steve Bartman was as rabid a Cubs fan as the next, and then if that wasn't enough, they actually attacked his family and friends, too.

What kind of nonsense is that? Were there any parents teaching their kids to be nice to someone who was as big a fan as they were? Did his error in judgment cause the Cubs to lose the NLCS that year? Have Cubs fans forgiven Steve Bartman? Why not? He was the bigger man and offered an apology.

If I was a betting man, I'd bet it took the 2016 championship to help people move forward and forgive Bartman. Forgiveness could have stopped the cycle of blame for why the Cubs hadn't consistently been a very good baseball team over the years. Instead of blaming the Curse of the Goat, Bartman or too many daytime games played in the hot sun, couldn't it have been possible the Cubs organization simply hadn't put together a good enough team to win the World Series?

Because one of the original definitions of the word forgiveness – which is similar to grace – is "to release, to hurl away, to free yourself," Cubs fans would have been less frustrated if they had forgiven Bartman and any other reason they clung to as to why the Cubs hadn't succeeded. As we all know, it's not that easy to forgive someone in our lives. However, the only thing more difficult than forgiveness is the alternative, and that's the burden of carrying a grudge.

To illustrate, a teacher instructed her class to put a potato in a plastic bag for every person they refused to forgive. The bag was to be carried everywhere they went to illustrate the burden. For some, that's a lot of weight. Like Cubs fans, if we forgive and move on, life will be lighter and more enjoyable.[98]

Because we're human, we are going to make mistakes. When we do, we need to avoid another mistake by making it right through apology.

The third item welcome, but largely missing from sports, especially from the parent perspective, is compassion and how it can play a vital role in the youth sports world. If we can't give someone grace, or are able to apologize, are we at least capable of providing someone compassion?

Recently, I reminisced about a Saturday morning on a cool, fall day during junior high school. I'm not sure what triggered the memories, but they were quite vivid. I was riding my bike across town to find out who had made the final roster of our seventh-grade basketball team. I was thinking this was the big time. To be pursuing the possibility of playing for our school was something I had pictured since I was even younger, and I was eager to see who was selected. This was the first time I had to try out for a team where cuts were involved, and I was nervous. My friends badgered me, insisting I was a cinch to make the squad. I tried to downplay their certainty because the last thing I was taught by my parents was to be overconfident, only to feel foolish if my name was omitted.

During my ride, I looked back to the months leading up to the cut day. I mentally went through my training checklist. I had spent a multitude of practice hours on our triangle-shaped patio. Bushes, shrubs, and flowerpots forced me to work on ball handling. Repeated Mikan drills taught me the ins and outs of our old hand-made square wooden backboard perched on the side of the garage.

Dad and I had played countless games of horse, stirring up my competitive drive. Lastly, I religiously worked on shooting when I pictured myself as just about every NBA player you could imagine. I had given it my best, so I had nothing to worry about, right? Obviously, my stomach didn't know that because the butterflies were at full flutter. When my buddies and I parked our bikes outside of school, we headed indoors to find the list. We stumbled all over each other as we raced for position at the gym door. Would the names be in alphabetical order or in order of jersey number or position?

Frantically, I searched the list and finally found my name. It was even spelled correctly. Then I noticed around me, not all of my buddies were as excited. We had all talked about playing together, but Coach could keep only 15 players.

Mom and Dad had talked it over with me about the possible outcomes of this situation. Certainly, it was a possibility I might not make the team, and if that happened, they encouraged me to remember how important it was to remain humble and respectful of others in the process. That experience taught me a valuable lesson of satisfaction in reaching a goal, but also humility and compassion for others.

As I've grown, I've also come to understand what a coach goes through in making cuts in search of the best team. It's not easy when dealing with people. If you care, it will always be challenging. For those making cuts, perhaps the hardest part is dealing with those on the outside looking in. Most often, those people never have to cut someone, and they don't understand how much time is spent pondering the big picture before arriving at the final outcome. That day, my bike ride home brought mixed emotions. We all hurt for a while, but we moved forward, better off because we had experienced it all.⁹⁹

Here is another great example of compassion where the father stepped forward and demonstrated to his family what was the right thing to do. Except during the Super Bowl, when commercials are intended to be more entertaining, I'm not one who intently watches ads during a televised sporting event. I feel there are too many breaks in the action as it is. Sometimes that's my time to head for the bathroom or the kitchen to take care of more important business. Most of the time though, I'll flip through the channels during timeouts to see other contests that might be on, only to view as long as it takes for our game of choice to return to live action.

One of the basic fundamentals of advertising is to educate the viewers of new or improved products/services and what these products or services can do for us. Recently a sports-related commercial caught my eye because of what takes place during the ad, but I wasn't able to recall the company, or the product being advertised. When you can't recall the company or product being advertised, but remember what takes place, it's a little more difficult to research what the commercial was all about. Nonetheless, by being able to explain to others what took place in the commercial, I was reminded it was a Toyota Tundra ad with the tagline "Let's go places."

In this particular spot, the closing moments of a high school football playoff game unfold when an official calls the receiver out-of-bounds on what would have been the winning touchdown. Obviously, the featured family and their son, one of the players, are dejected about the results. On the rainy ride home, they happen to come across the same official on the side of the road trying to get his broken-down car started. Still wearing his officiating uniform, the family recognizes him and, despite their disappointment from the game, the father stops to see if he needs a lift. He affirms he does and to help out, they make room.

The commercial finishes with the new tagline "Let's go compassion." I couldn't remember the company or the product because I was more focused on the compassion offered by the family. Despite their disappointment with the results of the game and the call this official made at the end, they did the right thing by being compassionate.

How many of us would do the same thing? How many of us would've believed it served him right? Should it matter if he makes a right or wrong call? Would we hesitate if he's wearing plain clothes and we don't recognize him? Compassion is the sympathetic pity and concern for the sufferings or misfortunes of others. This gentleman, who happened to be an official, experienced the fact his vehicle broke down during what turned out to be a stormy night. It shouldn't matter what took place earlier, but only that he needed help. It also doesn't matter what brand of vehicle we drive, because when someone is in need, compassion is something we can all give – from the heart.[100]

That's why I get excited when I see acts of good sportsmanship like what happened during 2016 opening weekend's college football games between Nebraska and Fresno State, and during the LSU-Wisconsin game. Wisconsin Badgers kicker Rafael Gaglianone wore jersey No. 27 during the contest and when I first saw it, the significance of him wearing that number didn't mean anything to me. I remembered he wore No. 10 the year before but didn't think much more of it. As it turned out, he wore No. 27 all season in honor of former Nebraska punter Sam Foltz, who died in a vehicle accident earlier that summer.

Gaglianone and Foltz became great friends over the prior three years while working together at kicking camps. The University of Nebraska football program took their opportunity a step further to show their respect toward Foltz. On their first offensive series, they went three and out (which may have been by design) and sent out the punting team. However, in honor of Foltz, they all lined up where they were supposed to, except they didn't have a punter standing where Foltz would have been. They then took a delay of game penalty, so Huskers fans could cheer and pay their appreciation to Foltz. Fresno State cooperated by declining the penalty and allowing Nebraska to send in Foltz's successor as they moved forward.

For obvious reasons, we don't want to have these types of gracious gestures taking place every week, but this thoughtfulness is something our kids should carry out towards our kids' teammates, opponents, and opposing parents at every opportunity. If you knock someone down, help them up. When you get beat soundly, congratulate the winner. As the victor, treat your opponent with respect and dignity.[101] Parents, congratulate all the kids for a game well played. Win or lose, reach out to the opponents' parents to strike a chord of community, because the game is over and it's time to act like parents, who are adults that get along.

Sportsmanship can be simple acts of kindness, or well-designed plans of affection. Nonetheless, if we continue to work to make sure good sportsmanship is the norm instead of the exception, the results will be an exciting development, too – just like a well-played game.

Chapter 14

Priorities & Perspective

When our children lose a contest, who feels worse, them or us? On one occasion after my kids experienced a tough setback the night before, I woke up and felt like I played the game myself. We need to keep perspective, remember our kids play games, and be thankful for their opportunities.

I read a story where a tiny West African town in Adare, Niger had received a new cement well. One of the women in the small town shouted, "Now we have everything." At the time of the story, Adare had no electricity, they gathered their water in buckets, and the town had one television run by a generator. Because the well's walls were no longer mud, their water was clear. They had everything! These people had proper perspective. For them, clear water was important.

The mere fact our kids are able to play ball, wrestle or swim should be most important. The results are extra. I forget this as much as anyone does. I don't always have proper perspective, but I should – we all should.

During the week of Super Bowl XLV, Green Bay Packers kicker Mason Crosby was interviewed on Media Day. Crosby was fully aware of how many championships had been decided in the waning moments. Regardless, Crosby insisted if it came down to it, one kick wouldn't define his career. He felt kicking is what he does, but not who he is.

The same applies for our kids. Now and then, they may lose a game, a match, or a race, but that doesn't make them losers. We should be ecstatic as parents they are able to play – period. Being competitive is acceptable. Striving for excellence is important. However, they still play games.

Annie's Mailbox is the modern-day version of Anne Landers' old advice column. In one publication, proper perspective was offered in a short list. If we develop awareness like this collection of thoughts, leading to proper perspective, we'll realize we really do have everything:

- Be thankful for the clothes that fit a little too snug because it means you have enough to eat.
- Be thankful for the mess you clean up after a party, because it means you have been surrounded by friends.
- Be thankful for the taxes you pay because it means that you're employed.
- Be thankful that your lawn needs mowing, and your windows need fixing, because it means you have a home.
- Be thankful for your heating bill because it means you are warm.
- Be thankful for the laundry because it means you have clothes to wear.
- Be thankful for the space you find at the far end of the parking lot, because it means you can walk.
- Be thankful for the lady who sings off-key behind you in church because it means you can hear.
- Be thankful people complain about the government because it means we have freedom of speech.
- Be thankful for the alarm that goes off in the early morning hours, because it means you're alive.[102]

If taken seriously, these thoughts offered by Annie's Mailbox will help us as we travel through life, because quite often we get comfortable in our routine or set in our ways. However you want to look at things, bumps in the road can wake us up, get our attention, and change our lives – even if it's a little bit.

This very morning, did you feel honored and privileged to wake up and enjoy the day? Everyone's reality starts with that same opportunity. There are many more important things in life than to become an irate father and pound on the hockey glass until it breaks. Let's remember the grip on reality is being lost when parents drug the water of their child's opponent in a tennis match – all in the name of winning. Take note that its way out of line for fans to accost officials before, during or after a basketball game, because they feel their favorite players can do no wrong. All these choices take away from the importance of living for the moment and enjoying the games we, or our children, play.

Some people feel it's their right to be passionate about sports. I agree. However, when it causes us to cross the line of control, then we've lost perspective – we've forgotten what's most important.[103]

When listening to sports talk radio, you hear quite a few different perspectives on a variety of topics. For instance, we've heard over the years how analysts proclaim Michael Jordan as the best offensive basketball player ever, Kobe Bryant as the best scorer, and LeBron James as the best all-around hoops player ever. That is the perspective of a percentage of the population.

I disagree with these opinions, because when it comes to basketball, I place importance on aspects of the game someone else might not.

Each year, as the NFL Network unveils their annual list of the 100 best players, we see very few players ranked exactly as they were the year before. Why was someone like Peyton Manning ranked No. 1 in one list, but J.J. Watt in another? Why was Aaron Rodgers ranked No. 11 in one year's list, but second in another? Do they change that much from one year to the next?

If your favorite team has six players ranked one year in the Top 100, and it has less the next year, does that mean your team won't be as good? Conversely, if they have more, does that mean they'll be better? It would be unwise on our part, to take these rankings on face value and assume they are accurate without fail. Without knowing what all goes into the rankings, the list means very little. How is the NFL Network's process different from Sports Illustrated's? It becomes an educational exercise, where we need to find out what lies behind a ranking, a list, or an opinion. We need to ask questions.

We can formulate opinions on many different topics, but if we don't have something to back them, we may be offering a weak perspective.

When coaching, if we believe every game is a win-at-all cost proposition, that perspective will determine how strategy is set, practices are conducted, and substitution patterns established. Sports are wonderful for learning and discussing – if we approach with proper perspective.[104]

When I was young, it seemed the Green Bay Packers always played at noon on Sundays. What perspective does that convey? It means the Packers of the 70's weren't good enough to be featured in primetime very often, so neighborhood football games right after another noon Packers loss were regular events. We would play these either in the vacant lot behind my neighbor's house or at the end of our dead-end road next to the water tower. Never did we worry about having enough players.

These days, colleges have around 100 players on their rosters, high schools on average suit up 60 to 70 guys on Friday nights, and in normal NFL seasons, teams choose 45 on game day from a roster of 53. That's a large pool to select from.

Looking at the other end of the spectrum, what's the minimum number of players required to avoid a forfeit? In 11-player football, the rules require a minimum of seven players be available to meet line of scrimmage requirements, and in 8-player football it's 5. If a team can't provide at least this many players, it's a forfeit and the opposing team is declared the winner.

What would be the score, you ask?

If the game had already started and the team losing had to forfeit, the score would remain the same as it was at the time the game ended. If a team can't provide enough players for the start of the game, a score of 1-0 is recorded for college and high school games and 2-0 for professional games. Because I've been through it as a coach, believe me when I say it's a painful ordeal to have to forfeit a game, or even two.

What if a team decided to forfeit – as a favor to their opponent?

In October of 2014 in the state of Washington, a school shooting took place in a cafeteria. A Friday night rivalry game was scheduled to take place after completion of the school week. However, because of the tragic event resulting in two deaths, the game to decide a conference championship and a playoff top seed was rightfully cancelled.

This was supposed to be a battle for supremacy in the Wesco 3A North Division – a big game. A gesture of incredible compassion followed as opposing Oak Harbor head coach Jay Turner offered to forfeit the game against Marysville Pilchuck. The offer didn't come forth because Turner was a 1990 graduate of Pilchuck, but because as he stated, "It's the right thing to do. We had a meeting with our kids after school and then I talked with my coaches, and we were all in 100 percent agreement that it was the right thing to do." They backed up what they said, because after traveling more than an hour to Marysville, they spent the time they normally would have been playing attending a vigil and meeting with the Marysville team to offer support.

In other states, where high school playoff football is sometimes too serious of business, would a gesture like this come forth? I pray it would, but I also pray this is one test, no one ever has to take again.[105]

You would think, if people had proper perspectives in life, it would be easy to set our priorities. However, the more I walk through life, the more I see people having a difficult time setting priorities. When 80 percent of professional athletes are either broke or divorced within two years of retiring from sports, problems setting priorities exist.

The money made in pro sports is amazing, and even a player making the minimum salary should be able to set themselves up for quite a long time if they properly set their priorities. Not only do professional athletes make a lot of money, they have just about everything done for them. Someone takes care of all their equipment, plane tickets, meals on the road, rides to the visiting stadium, etc. Prioritizing to save as much money as possible while playing can provide many options after a career is over.

When Charles Schwab and the Bethlehem Steel Company were starting out in 1904, there were times when Schwab felt the company wasn't operating on all cylinders. He was sought out by a consultant who felt he could teach Schwab how to manage better – to set better priorities. Schwab said to the consultant, "If you can give us something to pep us up to do the things we already know we ought to do, I'll gladly listen to you and pay you anything you ask." The consultant convinced Schwab he could give him something in 20 minutes that would increase the production of Bethlehem Steel by at least 50 percent. The consultant pulled a plain 3x5-note card from his pocket and advised Schwab to write down the six most important tasks for the next day. Three minutes later, the consultant commanded Schwab to put the tasks in order of importance – to prioritize them. After 5 more minutes, the consultant continued to explain to Schwab that he should save the card in his pocket, pull it out first thing in the morning and start working on No. 1. He was instructed to continue to focus on No. 1 until it was done, and then move on to No. 2, and so on. He told Schwab not to be concerned if he didn't finish the list in one day, because at least he was working on the most important tasks. However, the consultant did instruct Schwab to take the last 5 minutes of every working day to make out the new priority list for the next day. When the consultant was finished, he advised Schwab to try out his suggestions and then decide its value. Schwab implemented the advice of the consultant and five years later, the Bethlehem Steel Company was the biggest independent steel producer in the world. As it turned out, he paid the consultant $1,000 per minute for the advice that would generate hundreds of millions of dollars.

Being able to prioritize is an important thing for all of us to learn, because meaningful priorities bring rewarding lives.[106]

If a youth coach could be a present under the Christmas tree, parents should hope the main identifier of that gift would be character. I feel the standards for youth coaches should be different than those of professional coaches. Winning at all costs should not be part of a youth coach's job description. In youth sports – Little League through high school – coaches have such an incredible platform from which to influence kids. Parents need to allow their kids to be influenced by coaches who realize how important their task is, because most kids will hold on forever to memories about their youth coaches. The only question is whether those memories will be good or bad. Parents need for their kids' youth coaches to be full of character and enthusiasm – ones who do it the right way at all times.

Since actual playing days of childhood makes up a portion of life, parents need to identify coaching leaders whose main concern isn't winning at all costs on the field but teaching character and other life skills. They should be focused on helping train kids be the best they can be.

Sports and coaching provide a wonderful opportunity to demonstrate a great example to kids. When kids are older and look back, they won't remember how many contests they won, but they'll remember their coaches. A former player of mine started a youth program dedicated to teaching kids how to play the right way. When I asked him why he started it, he said it was because of the positive influence he received from a youth coach.

A coach can receive no greater praise, and like it or not, coaches have an incredible effect on a child's memories. Therefore, parents need to help their kids find youth coaches whose priority is to be a coach who provides fond memories.[107]

Paul Ihlenfeldt pointed out how kids can tell when coaches have genuine passion, because they're willing to run the hill with kids to demonstrate the value of prioritizing conditioning, and the importance of not giving up. He then commented how he would relate that activity to future employment, for days that would be tough and how they'd need to push through when those challenges arose in their lives. On the surface, running the hill may not be a fond memory, but it's a heck of a lot easier when a coach cares enough to demonstrate how pushing ourselves can be fun and a valuable priority in pursuing excellence in athletics as well as something valuable later in life.

My uncle was a Coast Guard cook during World War II, so when I was growing up, we were fortunate to experience some fancy treats. The aroma in his home at holidays was always special.

In his cottage, he had a free-standing chopping block for tenderizing meat or cutting fruits and vegetables. You always knew when he was preparing the next meal, not only because of the smells, but also because of the sounds on the chopping block.

In the world of college basketball, this chopping "sound" takes place after every season, but it's not nearly as pleasant as the kitchen analogy. There are thunderous cheers for the exciting upsets and finishes in the NCAA Tournament, but there's also the sound of the chopping block as coaches are fired after disappointing early departures.

Despite gaudy records over numerous years, conference championships and Final Four appearances, schools fire their successful coaches. Some schools dismiss their coaches after numerous seasons of at least 20 wins, guiding their teams to the school's first NCAA post-season win in many years. On paper, these examples demonstrate resumes' many schools would be proud to have. Apparently, these institutions have different priorities.

It also happens after each NCAA Tournament for successful coaches to receive offers from other schools after their team finishes the season. If that is the case, those coaches have to review priorities before making a decision.

If a major university decides to hire a "big-name" coach and basically establish a short-term feeding ground for the NBA, they have to decide what their priorities are surrounding the men's basketball program. Sadly, if priorities aren't set in proper order and followed accordingly, we can be led astray quite easily. Jobs, homes, vacations, and quiet time may all be on our list of importance, but what ranks first?

Prioritized lives will lead to rich, rewarding lives. They won't necessarily be full of wealth and fame, but when we have a purpose for living and learn to be content with what we have, we have greater wealth than we could imagine. When quality character isn't enough to lead a program, are our priorities mixed up? Some people believe material possessions should be our top priority, however wealth and luxury can make us over-confident, spoiled, and complacent. As parents, it's our job to choose priorities that last over what is temporary. This example demonstrates how choosing priorities is part of our lives, and how different people have different priorities.[108]

Nonetheless, whether we identify them as such or not, everyone has priorities in life. When Vince Lombardi was coach and general manager of the Green Bay Packers, he used to proclaim his priorities in life were faith, family, and football – in that order. When your priorities are aligned similarly, your life will consist of a focused, spirit-filled, family-oriented lifestyle first that doesn't leave room for too many other things. By watching where their greatest focus is in their lives, people should be able to determine their No. 1 priority. Too often, because of the behavior of parents and coaches, I'd be willing to bet Coach Lombardi's list of priorities are often being lived in reverse order.

With usually a zillion things going on in our lives, most people focus their attention on whatever pops up, until something else comes along. This isn't a recipe for success, but certain chaos. Quite often, this will lead us to choosing the path of least resistance, where we'll pick over the things we need to do and work on the easiest ones – leaving the more difficult and tedious tasks for later. However, quite often "later" never comes – or worse, comes right before the task needs to be completed, throwing us into panic mode filled with craziness, stress, and regret.

How should we set our priorities?

The first question we need to ask is what means the most to you? Vince Lombardi chose his faith as the most important thing in his life. Reportedly, he spent time every day dedicated to that faith. Everyone should have their family near the top of their list. In my opinion, if you don't have a faith to follow, your family should be Number 1. I also believe if your family isn't ranked Number 1 or 2, your family needs some immediate attention. The older I get, and the more times loved ones pass away, the more important family is to me.

When I watch high school football games, or any sport for that matter, and see how parents, coaches and/or players act as if the game is a life-or-death proposition, I conclude their priorities are mixed up. Again, these contests are meant to be fun. If they're not, someone's priorities are out of kilter.

In the business world, we can set our priorities for tomorrow by taking a few minutes each day when we're ready to go home and write down the six most important tasks for the following day's work hours.

When that simple task is completed, the assignments should be prioritized. Making sure the list is attacked in order and abiding by this easy-to-establish habit will produce daily priorities and soaring productivity. Establishing the same priorities as Coach Lombardi may not allow much time in our lives for other activities, but at least we'd be able to remember the short list and its order.[109]

On the other hand, if we had to focus on one priority, that would be honoring our family through relationships.

When NFL offseason practices get underway, teams work on getting to know their new players. Whether it's rookies, free agents or those obtained in a trade, the teams successful in working with the new guys will do better when the season rolls around. Often, even before he starts throwing passes, Green Bay Packers quarterback Aaron Rodgers mentions how he does his best to get to know his new team members, because triumphant relationships lead to more victories on the field.

Rodgers has even stated how he researches likes and dislikes of new players, so he can do his part in making the newbies feel at home. Why is that important? Rodgers wants the confidence levels of all his teammates to be high, so their questions and learning of the plays will be the best they can be and subsequently, so will the Packers. For success in sports and in life, positive relationships are paramount.

According to lifeoptimizer.org, here are five reasons why relationships should be our top priority:

- **Relationships fulfill your most important need of all.** The most important thing people need isn't money or achievements or recognition. The most important thing people need is love. We all need to love and be loved. Unfortunately, sometimes we're so obsessed with other things we forget how beautiful it is to love and be loved.

- **Relationships are the place where your greatest joy comes from.** One inseparable part of relationships is giving. Without giving, there is no genuine relationship. Whether it's time, attention, money or just a smile, genuine relationships are all about giving.

- **Only through relationships can you give lasting impact to others.** Which piece of advice will you honor more, the one from someone you don't really know, or the one from someone you love? We appreciate the people we love more than anyone else. Their words sink deep into our heart, not just our mind. That's why it's important to build lasting relationships.

- **Through relationships you have the people to support you in times of trouble.** When we face difficult times, we need other people to support us. No one can take care of everything by himself. When the world looks dark and the problem looks big, nothing is more valuable than the support of people we love. They encourage us to persevere, they accompany us in the time of trouble and they're willing to share the burden with us.

- **Eventually, relationships are the only things that matter.** When people are dying, they don't think about their achievements and awards. They don't care whether they are rich or famous. All those things become meaningless when people are facing the end. All they want is having the people they love around them. They want the warmth of love to be with them in their last moments.[110]

Are relationships high on your priority list?

Conclusion

It's true, we go through crazy times, but if it's not one thing in our life, it'll be defined by something else. Regardless of our situations, we need to make the best of them, determining what will be the benefits of those situations. Will we be more appreciative of our families? Will we be more grateful about our kids having the opportunity to play sports? What if school programs have to make some very tough decisions? In fact, Tim Bannon commented, "It could very well be that some scholastic sports will have to be cut back. It's already happened with some colleges, and as budgets get crunched, some of the school sports programs are going to go, and when they go, what's going to fill that void?" Bannon went on to say private, pay-to-play club sports could become the norm, which would create issues of inequity, where the pay-to-play system would reign over diminishing school, recreation, pick-up, and schoolyard sports. He felt it was ironic nowadays how a young athlete would probably have a better chance of competing by biking to a local public golf course and putting down $10 to play a round, than to find a pick-up baseball, basketball, or football game somewhere. His concern would then be that this inequity could create mental and psychological problems for those who wouldn't be able to afford to participate in the pay-to-play model, especially in the inner city. Are we ready for the possibility of having to move to that model? Will we be able to display good sportsmanship in any environment?

No matter what our challenge looks, acts, or feels like, how do we remove poor sportsmanship from youth sports parents? Can we return youth sports to a simple environment of fun? Is there too much money involved? Bannon feels we won't be able to actually get back to the way it used to be in youth sports. He stated so many things have changed, where kids are on their phones and devices, and they're not wandering out at the park, even caring about the valuable creativity opportunities in sports that others have mentioned. "It doesn't mean we can't de-escalate organized sports, and encourage all participants in sports, including individual sports," Bannon commented. He also said, "I think the main thing we need to do is make people aware of what's happening and try to get communities more involved to develop programs that are more inclusive, and to get parents to be an advocate for change, as they're a key element, and to get parents involved when their kids are little."

Scott Venci isn't sure what it will take to de-escalate the environment surrounding youth sports, but he reiterated he isn't fond of the social media environment accessible to everyone, including parents and athletes, and how often, on whatever platform is used, verbal wars go back and forth. This isn't productive progress towards positive change.

Could the media help change the sportsmanship environment surrounding youth sports? As Venci goes on to explain, he feels they could, but it's a difficult situation, because high school sportswriters are expected to find stories of young talent, and parents constantly reach out to them because they want their "budding" (according to the parents) child to have an article written about them. If the writer complies with the wish, are they unintentionally feeding into the very environment we're trying to change? Is the only real way for the media to stop feeding into the hype, by not covering it? Let's be clear, as long as the sportswriters are completing their mission without bias and prejudice, they aren't doing anything wrong.

Therefore, who is it up to? "What it comes down to, is it's up to the parents – to raise their kids well," said Venci. "Sportsmanship can get better, but it needs to start with parents, and they've got to get better, before we can expect kids to get better."

When addressing some of these same parents during my speaking travels, there are times I've wondered *myself* if positive change in youth sports is even taking place. Are we actually reaching anybody out there? Are we planting any good seeds?

The answer is "yes" to both questions, and here is a fond example of how planting positive seeds can affect a family and a community.

I've always contended people *can* change, and it does happen — sometimes right around us. After a presentation at a high school's athletic code meeting, a mother was waiting for me at the bottom of the stage. I had just finished speaking and was collecting my materials. I could tell she was anxiously waiting to say something. Honestly, my first thought was, *Oh oh, what did I say?*

It turns out, during the prior spring, I had spoken to her community's preseason Little League baseball meeting. The president of the league had informed me certain sets of parents were acting selfishly, and their out-of-line behavior was giving the community a bad name. He hoped some proactive work would cure their league of the developing trend of bad sportsmanship. It so happened, this woman and her family attended that meeting along with several hundred other people. My presentation dealt with sportsmanship fundamentals, and she felt I was directly speaking to them. She even commented how they slumped down in their chairs because it had become clear they were guilty of some pretty poor behavior.

After that first presentation, they went home and sat down as a family to make some changes. Until that time, they had created some unrealistic expectations for their son and the pressure was evident in his behavior. He was desperately trying to please his parents, but when he couldn't, his actions embarrassed his community, his team, *and* his family. Figuratively speaking, the name on the back of his jersey had become more important than the name on the front.

How do we help our kids, and in turn, ease up on them?

Adjust your expectations and allow the kids to play the game. Let them develop, let them learn and support them in a way that's calming. Let them fail, too, because kids are challenged by losses and mistakes. This family began cheering for all kids on the team, not just their son. This way they became involved with the entire program and displayed a caring attitude for others.

Lastly, they always demonstrated good sportsmanship. They

avoided the emotional outbursts of the past and the accompanying black eye of embarrassment. They wanted to set a positive, contagious example for all.

These simple changes brought a year full of peace and confidence-building they had never seen before.

As we discussed their journey, it brought a smile to all our faces, that I wouldn't change one bit.[111]

Scripture tells us not to repay anyone evil for evil, and to be careful to do what is right. Therefore, as it depends on us, living at peace with everyone. What does that look like in practical terms? Survivors of the early 1960's Fidel Castro regime learned not to fear, not to hate, and not to harm. In other words, learning not to fear infers we develop boldness and courage. Learning not to hate means we should focus on love, forgiveness, and grace, and learning not to harm implies a commitment to non-violence and love for others.

Parents, in the world of youth sports, it comes down to this: **S**ports **C**reates **O**pportunities to **R**espect and **E**ncourage. What role will you play in improving the sportsmanship environment surrounding youth sports? Because when sportsmanship prevails – we all **SCORE**.

Our vision should be as follows: To develop a spirit in sport where victory is not measured so much on the scoreboard, as it is in the stands and on the benches; where children, teens and adults can celebrate victory or defeat with style, grace, and sportsmanship; developing character for success in life.

Endnotes

Chapter 2 – Control

1. National Safety Council – The National Safety Council is America's leading nonprofit safety advocate. They focus on eliminating the leading causes of preventable injuries and deaths.
2. Center for Disease Control and Prevention (CDC) – The nation's health protection agency that works to save lives and protect people from health, safety, and security threats.
3. Tim Bannon, Special to the Milwaukee Journal Sentinel, "I Just Want to Play: $10 Billion Youth Sports Industry Powers Ahead Through the Pandemic Largely Unregulated", September 11, 2020.
4. Pixar Animation Studios, Walt Disney Pictures, "Monsters, Inc.", released November 2, 2001.
5. Bill Gosse, Green Bay Press-Gazette, "Fine Line Separates Good, Bad Sports", June 7, 2008.
6. Bill Gosse, Green Bay Press-Gazette, "Sportsmanship Starts with Look in Mirror", December 27, 2008.

Chapter 3 – Respect

7. Bill Gosse, Green Bay Press-Gazette, "We Should Return to Respect of Past", January 18, 2014.
8. Bill Gosse, Green Bay Press-Gazette, "It's Respect, Not the Result, that Matters", February 21, 2015.
9. Bill Gosse, Green Bay Press-Gazette, "Showing Respect not Just for Sports", June 6, 2010.
10. Bill Gosse, Green Bay Press-Gazette, "Coaches Must Show Respect When Game is in Hand", December 29, 2012.

11.   Bill Gosse, Green Bay Press-Gazette, "Don't Rely on Classic TV for Life Lessons", April 5, 2014.
12.   Bill Gosse, Green Bay Press-Gazette, "Let's Make Disrespect Unacceptable", March 12, 2017.
13.   Bill Gosse, Green Bay Press-Gazette, "Learn to Make the Best of Good, Bad, and Ugly", September 13, 2009.

Chapter 4 – Follow-up and Follow-through

14.   Bill Gosse, Green Bay Press-Gazette, "Sportsmanship only Works with Proper Follow-Through", December 13, 2009.
15.   Bill Gosse, Green Bay Press-Gazette, "Follow-Through when You See a Teachable Moment", October 5, 2013.
16.   Bill Gosse, Green Bay Press-Gazette, "Follow-Up on Sportsmanship Goals", March 19, 2016.

Chapter 5 – Patience

17.   Bill Gosse, Green Bay Press-Gazette, "Patience can Pay Off – Eventually", November 13, 2015.
18.   Bill Gosse, Green Bay Press-Gazette, "Patience is Really a Virtue", October 16, 2016.
19.   Kyra M. Newman, www.mindful.org, "The Benefits of Being a Patient Person, April 5, 2016.

Chapter 6 – Letting Kids Make Mistakes

20.   Bill Gosse, Green Bay Press-Gazette, "Like the Butterfly, We Need Hurdles to Overcome", April 5, 2009.
21.   Bill Gosse, Green Bay Press-Gazette, "Dad's Letter Shows True Worth of Sport", February 27, 2016.
22.   Life Skills International and its affiliates are a 501©3 non-profit educational organization that is dedicated to giving individuals the information and support necessary to break free from destructive behavior patterns.

23. Bill Gosse, Green Bay Press-Gazette, "We Can Benefit from Mistakes", July 2, 2011.

Chapter 7 – Virtues and Values

24. This refers to 2 Thessalonians 3:13, where it challenges us to keep going on the right path, no matter what happens to us in life.

25. Bill Gosse, Green Bay Press-Gazette, "Values Should Drive Behavior", November 27, 2015.

26. Josephson Institute of Ethics, located in Playa del Rey, CA, is a 501©3 non-profit educational organization that is working to create a world where decisions and behavior are guided by ethics. They are recognized for their Six Pillars of Character (Appendix A).

27. MomsTeam.com is the website for MomsTeam Institute, Inc., a 501©3 non-profit, which is a youth sports resource for parents seeking advice and information, as they work to make sure youth sports is safe for all children ages 3 to 23.

28. Bill Gosse, Green Bay Press-Gazette, "Winning at all Costs is a Hollow Victory", December 27, 2009.

29. Bill Gosse, Green Bay Press-Gazette, "List of Values Worth More than End of Year Countdowns", January 4, 2014.

30. This passage comes from Matthew 5:10, which is part of The Beattitudes Jesus presented in his Sermon on the Mount.

31. Bill Gosse, Green Bay Press-Gazette, "Encourage Leaders to Follow Convictions", February 6, 2016.

32. Bill Gosse, Green Bay Press-Gazette, "Like Indiana, We can't let Bad Sports off the Hook", March 1, 2008.

33. Bill Gosse, Green Bay Press-Gazette, "Doing the Right Thing is Picture Perfect", April 9, 2011.

34. Bill Gosse, Green Bay Press-Gazette, "Winning Means Nothing without Dignity, Class", July 19, 2009.

35. Bill Gosse, Green Bay Press-Gazette, "In the Heat of the Moment, What do You do?", March 2, 2013.

36. Bill Gosse, Green Bay Press-Gazette, "Doing Right more Important than Winning", June 1, 2013.

37. Bill Gosse, Green Bay Press-Gazette, "Ten Tips for the Parents of Young Athletes", December 7, 2013.

38. Bill Gosse, Green Bay Press-Gazette, "Like Jeter, be a Shining Light for Others", August 2, 2014.

Chapter 8 – Humility

39. This passage comes from Matthew 5:5, which is also part of The Beattitudes Jesus presented in his Sermon on the Mount.

40. Bill Gosse, Green Bay Press-Gazette, "Humility Should be every Leader's Goal", July 11, 2015.

41. Bill Gosse, Green Bay Press-Gazette, "Humility can go a Long Way", October 23, 2016.

42. Bill Gosse, Green Bay Press-Gazette, "Don't Set up Kids for a Big Fall Later in Life", April 4, 2010.

43. This "ancient proverb" comes from the Book of Proverbs 25:27.

44. Bill Gosse, Green Bay Press-Gazette, "Humility is not a Sign of Weakness", July 19, 2014.

45. Bill Gosse, Green Bay Press-Gazette, "Stay Humble and Stay Hungry", October 4, 2008.

46. Bill Gosse, Green Bay Press-Gazette, "Humility can go a Long Way", October 23, 2016.

47. Bill Gosse, Green Bay Press-Gazette, "Great Athletes stay Humble, Hungry", December 5, 2015.

Chapter 9 – Encouragement

48. This "ancient proverb" comes from the Book of Proverbs 18:21.

49. Bill Gosse, Green Bay Press-Gazette, "If Nothing Else, Let's provide Kids with Hope", February 28, 2010.

50. Bill Gosse, Green Bay Press-Gazette, "Words should Inspire, not Hurt", January 19, 2008.

51. This story came from a daily devotional provided by Bible Gateway (biblegateway.com).

52. Bill Gosse, Green Bay Press-Gazette, "Choosing Kind Words can make Lasting Impact", October 11, 2009.

53. Bill Gosse, Green Bay Press-Gazette, "Praise can be Powerful Motivator", December 6, 2014.

54. Bill Gosse, Green Bay Press-Gazette, "The Power of Encouragement is Amazing", January 1, 2016.

55. Bill Gosse, Green Bay Press-Gazette, "In Life, make a Difference to One", April 9, 2016.

56. Bill Gosse, Green Bay Press-Gazette, "Empower, don't Embarrass", May 24, 2014.

57. Bill Gosse, Green Bay Press-Gazette, "Anyone can affect History", September 6, 2008.

58. Bill Gosse, Green Bay Press-Gazette, "Encouragers make good Things happen", May 31, 2014.

Chapter 10 – Sports Should be Fun

59. Bill Gosse, Green Bay Press-Gazette, "Summer Formula Works if Everyone stays Cool", April 19, 2009.

60. Bill Gosse, Green Bay Press-Gazette, "Parents should back off, let Kids Play", December 8, 2007.

61. Bill Gosse, Green Bay Press-Gazette, "Summer Games all about Fun", July 14, 2012.

62. Bill Gosse, Green Bay Press-Gazette, "Journey Starts with Lots of Smiles at T-Ball", May 24, 2009.

63. Bill Gosse, Green Bay Press-Gazette, "Parents should back off, let Kids Play", December 8, 2007.

64. Bill Gosse, Green Bay Press-Gazette, "Forget the Stars, Kids just want Chance to Play", November 22, 2009.

65. Bill Gosse, Green Bay Press-Gazette, "Let Kids Play for the Right Reason", August 18, 2007.

66. Bill Gosse, Green Bay Press-Gazette, "Let Kids Play Multiple Sports", September 15, 2007.

67. Bill Gosse, Green Bay Press-Gazette, "Don't let Clubs dampen Thrill of Prep Sports", November 24, 2007.

68. Bill Gosse, Green Bay Press-Gazette, "Imagine Fans Watching all Games in Peace", April 26, 2009.

Chapter 11 – Parental Support

69. Bill Gosse, Green Bay Press-Gazette, "Don't let Stress ruin the Ballpark Experience", May 14, 2011.
70. Bill Gosse, Green Bay Press-Gazette, "Handle Stress; Don't Pass it On", October 18, 2008.
71. Bill Gosse, Green Bay Press-Gazette, "Athletics should be safe Haven, not Field for Guilt", February 22, 2009.
72. Bill Gosse, Green Bay Press-Gazette, "Kids shouldn't need Bricks to get Our Attention", October 11, 2008.
73. Bill Gosse, Green Bay Press-Gazette, "Athletics should be safe Haven, not Field for Guilt", February 22, 2009.
74. Bill Gosse, Green Bay Press-Gazette, "Adults could Learn a Bit from the Family Dog", July 6, 2013.
75. Dr. Josh Axe, Adidas Runtastic, "Five Ways Stress Effects your Body", June 10, 2020.
76. Bill Gosse, Green Bay Press-Gazette, "We are getting Away from 'Let Kids be Kids'", June 16, 2014.
77. Bill Gosse, Green Bay Press-Gazette, "Parents can ruin the Fond Memories of Youth", October 25, 2009.
78. Bill Gosse, Green Bay Press-Gazette, "It's Sad when Parents can't keep Sports in proper Focus", June 17, 2012.
79. Bill Gosse, Green Bay Press-Gazette, "Kids best Interests often take Back Seat", June 28, 2014.
80. Bill Gosse, Green Bay Press-Gazette, "Balance Important in, out of Sports", November 27, 2016.
81. Bill Gosse, Green Bay Press-Gazette, "Right kind of Support for Athletes begins at Home", July 11, 2010. This section includes information from the former website essortment.com.
82. Bill Gosse, Green Bay Press-Gazette, "Growing up is about More than just Money", August 1, 2015.

Chapter 12 – Gratitude vs Entitlement

83. Bill Gosse, Green Bay Press-Gazette, "It's our Job to say Thank You", October 14, 2012.

84. Carrie D. Clarke, www.nextlevelcoachconsult.com, "The Thrive Global Community", 2018.

85. Bill Gosse, Green Bay Press-Gazette, "Grateful for crack of Bat, Roar of Crowd", May 21, 2016.

86. Bill Gosse, Green Bay Press-Gazette, "Count Blessings, not Setbacks", October 25, 2008.

87. Bill Gosse, Green Bay Press-Gazette, "It's a Privilege to play for Your School Team", August 4, 2007.

88. Bill Gosse, Green Bay Press-Gazette, "Parents can take Page from Selfless Examples", September 12, 2010.

89. Bill Gosse, Green Bay Press-Gazette, "Not Everyone should wear 'Elite' Label", June 7, 2009.

90. Bill Gosse, Green Bay Press-Gazette, "There are no Guarantees", July 5, 2008.

91. Bill Gosse, Green Bay Press-Gazette, "Let Spirit of Thanksgiving Live on Every Day", November 28, 2010.

92. Bill Gosse, Green Bay Press-Gazette, "Be Grateful in Sports, everyday Life", November 29, 2014.

Chapter 13 – Grace, Forgiveness and Compassion

93. Bill Gosse, Green Bay Press-Gazette, "Showing Grace is always the Right Move", September 13, 2014.

94. Bill Gosse, Green Bay Press-Gazette, "Sometimes, a little Grace goes a Long Way", September 14, 2013.

95. Bill Gosse, Green Bay Press-Gazette, "Showing Grace is always the Right Move", September 13, 2014.

96. Bill Gosse, Green Bay Press-Gazette, "Forgiveness is great Stress Reducer", August 6, 2016.

97. Bill Gosse, Green Bay Press-Gazette, "Apologies are necessary to Right Wrongs", October 23, 2011.

98. Bill Gosse, Green Bay Press-Gazette, "Forgiveness is great Stress Reducer", August 6, 2016.

99. Bill Gosse, Green Bay Press-Gazette, "Cut-down Day provided Lesson in Compassion", April 23, 2011.

100. Bill Gosse, Green Bay Press-Gazette, "Compassion makes the World Better", January 15, 2017.

101. Bill Gosse, Green Bay Press-Gazette, "Nebraska Punter Tributes show good in Sports", September 11, 2016.

Chapter 14 – Priorities and Perspective

102. Bill Gosse, Green Bay Press-Gazette, "Win or Lose, It all comes down to Perspective", February 20, 2011.

103. Bill Gosse, Green Bay Press-Gazette, "Life is too short to lose Perspective on Sports", April 18, 2015.

104. Bill Gosse, Green Bay Press-Gazette, "Sports are great, from a Proper Perspective", June 11, 2016.

105. Bill Gosse, Green Bay Press-Gazette, "Compassionate Forfeit puts Prep Football in Proper Perspective", November 1, 2014.

106. Bill Gosse, Green Bay Press-Gazette, "Prioritizing is an Important Lesson to Learn", August 31, 2013.

107. Bill Gosse, Green Bay Press-Gazette, "Winning isn't Top Priority for Youth Coaches", December 25, 2011.

108. Bill Gosse, Green Bay Press-Gazette, "Meaningful Priorities bring Rewarding Lives", March 31, 2013.

109. Bill Gosse, Green Bay Press-Gazette, "Put Priorities in Proper Order", September 25, 2015.

110. Bill Gosse, Green Bay Press-Gazette, "Relationships should be a Top Priority", May 28, 2016.

Conclusion

111. Bill Gosse, Green Bay Press-Gazette, "Positive Change can start at the Lowest Levels", August 9, 2008.

Appendix

Josephson Institute of Ethics Six Pillars of Character

Trustworthiness

- Be honest.
- Keep your promises.
- Be reliable — do what you say you'll do.
- Be loyal — stand by your family, friends, and country.

Respect

- Treat others with respect and follow the Golden Rule.
- Be tolerant and accepting of differences.
- Don't threaten, hit or hurt anyone.
- Deal peacefully with anger, insults, and disagreements.

Responsibility

- Do what you are supposed to do.
- Persevere.
- Do your best.
- Use self-control.

Fairness

- Play by the rules.
- Be open-minded; listen to others.
- Don't take advantage of others.
- Don't blame others carelessly.

Caring

- Be kind and compassionate.
- Express gratitude.
- Forgive others and show mercy.
- Help people in need.

Citizenship

- Do your share to make your home, school, community, and world better.
- Cooperate.
- Stay informed; vote.
- Be a good neighbor.